Out of
the River Mist

C. Raymond Clar

An authentic history of Guerneville, Sonoma County,
California, prior to the Great Depression,
as seen through the eyes of a native son.

C. Raymond Clar

A private edition limited to 400 copies,
clothbound, individually numbered
and signed.

Number: 346

"How different," I kept thinking,
*"is the present world of Doug,
Alan and Ric, Marcia and Anne."*

THE 10-year-old girl in the dark skirt, middie blouse and "pig-tail" hairdo stood beside her desk in the Santa Rosa parochial school that Monday morning. Her assignment was to describe the family week-end auto trip. Immediately behind her sat the petite, meek and shy Imelda Clar, a boarding student.

The speaker proceeded: "We drove past Gurney-ville to Jenner. Then we came back up the river and ate lunch at Gurney-ville —." A violent yank on the pig-tail from the rear pulled the speaker down in her seat. "No, no," shouted the meek and shy boarding student, "It's GURN-ville."

CONTENTS

Illustrations

(Continued next page)

CONTENTS (continued)

Foreword

Out of the fabric of childhood memories; out of the scraps of recorded writings and conversations with the elders; out of the drifting river mists I here attempt to reconstruct the village of my childhood. The result is by no means mere fantasy. Every stated incident is as factually correct as could be determined. The story is intended to be neither fully autobiographical nor chronologically historical. There was no intent of listing the names and character descriptions of all or of any particular citizens of the old town. The characters came forward as they quite incidentally seemed to be needed for the reconstruction of the village of my youth.

Most of the man-made structures and most of the living souls have long since drifted away in the inexorable flow of time and human destiny. Only the eternal hills and the grey-green river endure as a sort of perennially beautiful exoskeleton for the transient mayfly of human occupation.

The time and place of my youth were, I firmly believe, something unusual within the long, long calendar of decades marked out as Man's common journey on Planet Earth. This was especially true of technological changes with their consequent impact upon the broad society and culture to a degree not yet fully measured. I cannot conceive of any similar time period, past or future, when electricity, smashed atoms and skyrocket aircraft have, or could, replace wax candles, ox carts and saddle horses.

And, is it hoping too much to here recreate in word structures, woven out of gossamer threads of memory, that village culture which once was and which exists no more? Or will the result be only the stuff of drifting river mist? Should the reader grow weary of wandering along my undisciplined path toward that end, let us at least part with a mutual "Fare thee well, friend."

1

Green Twilight and Silence

GEOLOGISTS inform us that during the most recent convulsive stages in the stretching and folding of our coastal hills, the Russian River kept pushing its course westward toward the Pacific Ocean in spite of the rising mountains that tried to turn it back. These geologic convulsions caused the stream to twist and turn into numerous ox-bows. The Indians were impressed by this feature and named the river Shabaikai, the snake.

One particular ox-bow flowed north, probably into the floor of present Armstrong Grove, and then turned south, leaving Lone Mountain as a virtual island. Eventually, the river in flood stage cut through the top of the ox-bow U, and the river assumed its present course. Presumably this happened some five or six thousand years ago.

While the years followed one upon another into the centuries and millenia — as we earth people measure time — there was one living thing which prevailed against the persistent forces of change. The giant tree plant we call redwood did not go the way of the saber-tooth tiger and the woolly mammoth. At least three million years ago this ancient living thing was thriving in this moist coastal region.

After the waters ceased to flow around the old Big Bottom ox-bow, millions of tiny redwood seeds were blown from hillside trees, into the rich flats of the old river bed. Thousands took root. In a few centuries most of the competing tree, shrub and ground plants gave up the fight for existence in the deep shade of the high redwood forest.

As a professional forester, and as one who insists upon exposing historical facts with as much accuracy as human activities and observations may be reported, I dare to make this bold statement. I believe that on the Guerneville Big Bottom there once grew the most voluminous and the tallest body of living vegetable matter ever to have grown upon this earth at any place and at any time. There is reasonable documentary evidence upon which to base this thesis as well as the fact of ideal growth conditions for this particular plant species.

Down on the floor of the dense forest there was perpetual green twilight and silence. Seedling or sucker sprouts grew and grew as winter rain followed upon summer sun and fog. In the course of fifteen or twenty centuries of life the old trees would become weary and die and eventually fall. Young redwoods would crowd into the temporary deep well of sunlight, as would hazelnut, dogwood and other shade-enduring plant species.

But in the course of a few more centuries the new redwoods would have filled in the overhead canopy and once again the deep, green twilight would prevail on the silent spongy floor of the great forest. Only ferns, oxalis, some berries and a few other low plants could live and thrive in the tangle of litter and fallen tree trunks. Poison oak maintained life by stretching persistent tentacles up the rough tree trunk into the sunlit foliage.

Few moving ground creatures found a home here. Perhaps the racoons came when the clear streams were teeming with spawning fish; or perhaps a black bear. And a few squirrels undoubtedly traversed the Big Bottom by way of the airy foliage 300 feet above the ground. One scientist has referred to such dense forest as a "biological desert."

And then came Man, a new and disturbing mobile creature upon the face of the earth. Just when he first wandered into the Santa Rosa Valley and along our ocean shore is uncertain. Perhaps 5000 years ago; perhaps a thousand years earlier or later.

Travel into the isolated interior Russian River must have been as difficult for these aboriginal people as it was for their pale skinned successors upon the land.

Difficulty of travel throughout this area posed a problem even until the time of my own childhood.

The Pomo Indian People came and built numerous villages at the edge of the forest in the vicinity of present Sebastopol and Healdsburg, and all along the coast. These short, dark, very sturdy people lived richly on acorns, berries, small and large game and fish and waterfowl. On the coast they had a great plenty of seals, salmon, shell fish, kelp and plant seeds and roots. They excelled above all other Indian people in the weaving of basketry.

Where did they come from? Well, they were Earth People because their Common Ancestor was Old Man Coyote, and every-

4

one knew that the Great Spirit had created him from the Red Earth long, long ago.

The Pomo triblets enjoyed generally good relations with the Miwok people who lived from about Occidental and Duncan's Point southward. Occasionally there had been local disputes over hunting or acorn rights with the Wappo people who had forced their way across the River at Geyserville perhaps a thousand years ago.

The Coastal Pomo and the Interior Valley Pomo always maintained their relationship and a profitable exchange of commodity goods. From the ocean came dried kelp, dried fish and shell money. In the interior there was magnasite, elk horn for knives, and obsidian for arrow heads. Yew bow stock could be acquired from the northern Yu-kai people.

Students of ethnology have traced old Indian trails running westward from Geyserville and Cloverdale to the coast, and down around the redwood belt by Freestone and Bodega. I can find no record of routes generally through the Russian River mountain region. The Pomo were not boat builders. For the ocean surf they made rafts of a couple of logs; and they constructed tule raft-canoes at Clear Lake. There were no known Indian dugout canoes on the Russian River.

There is substantial evidence that a trail did generally follow the river along its northern bank. Between the village of Tcetcewani near Mirabel Park, and the village Chalanchawi, where Willow Creek meets the Russian River two miles inland there were two known substantial camp grounds or possibly permanent settlements. Across the river from Hollydale Park was the village of Budutcilan. And at present Guerneville was Ciole [See-oh-lay]. This latter name very significantly meant "shady place."

I feel quite certain that I know precisely where Ciole village or camp was located. I feel so because I think I lived on the spot from about my third to my fifteenth year. This was the grassy spot above the Catholic Church and around the Laws' home. Small as it was, this was about the only grassy glade that existed locally midst the heavy virgin forest. More important, it was not at all uncommon for one of us youngsters to pick up an arrowhead out in the grass. I remember very distinctly the day my brother

Clarence dug up an arrowhead not shaped like the others while he was digging around a small stump. The few redwood stumps there were all small and scattered.

So, the Pomo People lived their lives in what must have been a happy situation. Throughout the centuries trading or hunting parties probably passed by Ciole and camped for a few days or throughout the summer. It is likely that they enjoyed here an unusual freedom from human enemies or grizzly bear or rattlesnakes. Thus, we can assume that Guerneville's reputation as a summer recreation resort was established at a very early date.

It is likely, too, that the people spent little time in the deep twilight of the giant redwoods. There was no particular reason why they should have done so.

Very probably the Miwok people had told their Pomo neighbors about the coastal visit of Francis Drake in 1579, and Sebastian Cermeño in 1593, with their great white winged canoes. But these strange stories must have become vague legends by the time of the friendly visit of the Spaniards under Juan Francisco de Bodega y Cuadro in 1775 off present Bodega Bay.

By the year 1800 the native Indian people along the coast and in the Santa Rosa Valley must have been well aware of the gradual encroachment of the strange, pale skinned people around San Francisco Bay. But, as already stated, the mountainous Russian River area was very isolated.

And then it happened.

Let us imagine something like this. At dawn one spring day, several young men awoke and crawled out of their brush-thatched hut. They started down the trail to tend their gill nets set in a brush dam where the river narrowed around Neeley's Point. As they walked they chewed their breakfast of deer jerky. They wore no moccasins because the ground was not rough; and they wore hardly any other clothing. The chill of the crisp morning fog was hardly noticed by them. These people were completely at home with the weather and landscape around them.

As they waded into the stream to retrieve the trapped fish before some of the riverside animals beat them to it, several of the boys thought they heard something unusual.

6

"It was only a beaver slapping his tail," said the eldest.

And then out of the rising mist, approaching them up the river, came a strange canoe made of sewn skins. This was an Alaskan bidarka. In the canoe were several heavily bearded men with unusual facial features; and there were several Indians whose features were fully as strange to the Pomo boys. These were Aleuts who had come down the coast with the Russian fur hunters.

The intruders made signs of peace and spoke a few Pomo words of friendship. But the local youth fled like deer to report the news after they had recovered from their initial shock.

The year was — shall we say 1812; it could have been earlier — it does not matter. The ancient, isolated Shabaikai River of the Pomo People would never be the same again. The strange, white beaver trappers had come, and they called the river the Slavianka, which 'seems to have meant "the pretty little Russian girl." And they came often and set traps until the beaver became scarce. In 1841 the Russians abandoned Fort Ross and departed across the sea.

In the meantime, the Spanish Colony had persisted in Alta California for half a century. Missions were thriving and the several presidio and pueblo communities were well established, if not heavily populated. And then, soon after the Russian trappers appeared, Mexico became an independent nation. Upper California became a department or province in 1822.

In 1823 the last and the most northern missions were started at Sonoma and San Rafael. In 1833, young Sergeant Mariano Guadalupe Vallejo was instructed to explore the upper reaches of the Santa Rosa Valley and to visit and report upon the Russian stronghold on the coast. Vallejo related much later how he had erected a temporary presidio in April of 1833 at a place he called Juarez, where Mark West Creek met the Russian River, that is, near present Mirabel Park.

One year later Vallejo's brother-in-law, John B. R. Cooper, was persuaded to construct California's first commercial power driven sawmill at that very place.

Vallejo did visit Fort Ross, but he did not say how he traveled there from his temporary fort near Fulton. It is most likely that he took the easy way south around the Petaluma and Bodega open lands. He surely would have left a detailed record if his party had struck out westerly down the vague river trails.

At this time the Spanish called the river the San Ysidro and possibly San Sebastian. By about 1844 it was becoming commonly known as *El Rio Ruso;* and land grants were being settled as far north as the Sanel Rancho at present Hopland.

By the time of the American Conquest in 1846, lumbering had become a rather substantial industry in the redwood region around Bodega, at Corte Madera in Marin County, in the Oakland hills, and throughout the Santa Cruz Mountains. The old method of whip-sawing boards by hand was being supplanted by numerous water powered mills. And the first stationary steam engine, probably west of the Mississippi River, was brought around the Horn by Steven Smith and put to sawing lumber at Bodega in 1844.

But the isolated Russian River redwoods were not disturbed. Under the great trees there was still the pale light of green twilight, and there was still the awesome silence.

And so, a very small number of Man creatures plodded along on foot on the littered floor of the great forest and across the few grassy hillsides sometimes called "glades." As the meandering trails made by large wild animals became more easily traversed because of Man's repeated use, saddle horses could become the prime carriers.

Russian trappers must have relied almost entirely on their skin covered canoes for movement along the river. And they surely penetrated the major tributary streams on foot as far as beaver dams were to be found. Who knows where the wraithlike Indians had not wandered during their centuries of living with the pleasant land; passing lightly as the autumn leaves.

The rivers were the natural transportation arteries of the vast wild continent. And that is one reason why the earliest tie, a sort of commercial umbilical cord, between the interior Russian River and the developing new American State was by way of Healdsburg rather than Santa Rosa.

The other reason appears to me to have been the logical progress of redwood timber exploiters around the shoulder of Mt. Jackson. Consider, for example, that remarkable pioneer, John

Washington Bagley. Soon after his Mexican War service he found himself working in the East Bay redwoods in the vicinity of Moraga. Then he moved up into the bitter squatter battlefield of Mill Creek, west of Healdsburg. That was probably about the time the Civil War started. Then by war's end he was on the Big Bottom with others, as will be mentioned later. There, it was claimed, he ran the log carriage into the saw with the first log sawed. Many other lumbering pioneers of Guerneville also came to this place by way of Healdsburg.

In respect to transportation upon the small and wandering river, there is evidence of hope and trial, if not success. Apparently, a number of downriver rafts carried provisions from Healdsburg to Guerneville without mishap. Julia Guerne left a note telling of her father on such a raft being nearly swamped after striking a log. The Duncans rafted some logs to their sawmill near the river mouth.

Miss Guerne obviously was informed that the dreamer of grand dreams, Captain John M. King, built the shallow draft Steamer *Enterprise* at Guerneville and not at Duncans, as otherwise reported. This was probably accomplished in 1874. Julia noted: "King built the first steamboat . . . in Guerneville near Tom Pippin's edger. He made his first trip as far as Murphy and Brackett Mill [near Rio Nido]. The next day they reached the mouth of Green Valley Creek where they stranded and Roscoe Longley had to pull them out by ox team." Whatever the truth of the several versions of the story, the steamboat on the Russian River was not a success. *

---

*See *"Fiasco, or the Steamboat on the Russian River,"* by Helen Lightfoot, in Sonoma County Historical Journal. *Winter 1971. Santa Rosa.*

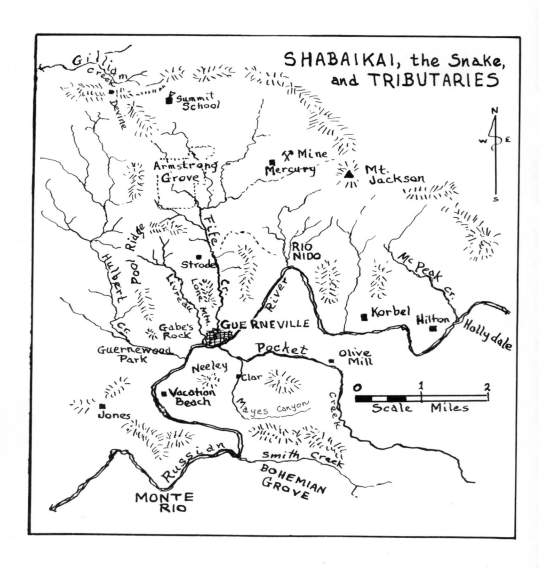

Sketch map of the Russian River and its major tributary streams in the vicinity of Guerneville. Such rough and twisted topography caused unusual difficulty in constructing railroads and highways. It also accounts for the isolation of the early day interior river settlements.

2

The First Homesteaders

THE native Pomo Indians had departed from the interior river country as quietly as the drifting winter mist. I have never heard of or seen any evidence of their presence except for the few stray arrowheads. It is doubtful if any Russian trapper paddled upon the river after 1840.

Who were the very first of the aggressive American land seekers to venture down or up the river into these hinterlands? It is repeatedly stated that R. B. Lunsford was the first to settle at present Guerneville. This he did on May 1st, 1860. I have read that statement in a reputable county history printed in 1880, and I assume that was the first printed record of the alleged fact.

We should first consider some major conditions affecting the original permanent claiming of specific land parcels in this particular isolated region. This was, of course, a practice entirely foreign to Indian community sharing of the land and its resources. Gold was not the magnet drawing the restless immigrants from Eastern States into Sonoma County. Other minerals were rare and too uncertain to attract any except far roving prospectors. Most of the beaver were trapped out, although my father remembered having seen a few. He first visited the area in 1877 at the age of nineteen, when Rio Nido was being logged.

Two other obvious resources must have been responsible for attracting permanent settlers or opportunists. Claimants could have sought to establish family subsistence agricultural homesteads. Or they could have quite logically desired to claim a quarter square mile of fine redwood timber.

Strange as it now seems, to acquire the latter the homesteader did in fact have to knowingly falsify his sworn record of claim. There was no simple legal vehicle for purchasing government timber nor for making a homestead claim other than for grazing or cultivating the land. And in the latter case the claimant was required to attest that he was a resident upon the land.

Equally guilty with the numerous dubious claimants was the Congress of the United States and the legislature of this and the

11

other western States. Those bodies could not or would not forcefully solve the complex problems associated with any practical disposition of the public domain, and especially the forested vacant land. That is a very complicated story. Yet without some comprehension of the prevailing conditions, any attempt to search out and name the first non-Indian settlers upon specific land parcels would be most difficult.

The Gold Rush and consequent population increase caused a great demand for lumber products in central California. Milled material was shipped around Cape Horn from the Eastern Seaboard. The Puget Sound sawmills enjoyed their first great economic boom. Little mills sprang up in the foothills of the Sierra and wherever redwood timber was most available. North of the Santa Cruz Mountains this meant the inner edge of the redwood forest in Marin County and the west side of the Santa Rosa Valley. It also meant the Mendocino seacoast and near the mouth of the Russian River. The quality of lumber is a very secondary matter compared with the problem of getting it to the destination of use.

The above descriptive paragraph relates to the repeated reference to the isolated position of the noble redwood forest of the Big Bottom. And that is why the eventual coming of the railroad was such an important event, and why the desperate try was made for transport by steamboat on the river.

So consider, now, the ambitious immigrant from another State who pushes his way by foot, or on horseback or boat into the interior Russian River with the hope of making a permanent home or a small fortune in lumber. The trail along the ocean from Bodega to the Gualala River had been used for decades by Indians, Spaniards, Mexican *Californios,* Russians and *Anglos.* This was in effect The Czar's Highway for twenty years. At any rate, it could have been used as a logical point of entry to the interior river. From the other direction, downriver Indian trails must have been clearly marked, if somewhat difficult in places.

And it is not at all impossible that the immigrant American had made his journey west from Healdsburg, up Mill Creek, and over The Ladder. Then he could work his way southwesterly across the tumbled westward drainages of Gray Creek and Gilliam Creek

12

until he reached the summit of the Jackson Range. From there he could have looked down as the eagle looked upon the tops of the great, dense redwoods of the Big Bottom.

But when he arrived, where was he in point of reference? If he were standing to the north or west of the general course of the twisting river, and if the year was later than 1855, he could assume that he stood in Sonoma and not in Mendocino County. The particular political township would be uncertain. Of course, there were no section corners until late 1866. About the only certain condition was the lack of any possible quarrel as to whether his desired land was in an affirmed Mexican land grant, such as would have prevailed in the Santa Rosa Valley. No such grants extended into these mountains.

The first land claimant of record on the Big Bottom was very likely not the first settler upon the land in the general vicinity. The first recording that I can identify with the location was filed by William Henry Willits. Willits had arrived in California in 1853 from the State of Illinois. How he traveled into the Big Bottom we do not know. Nor do I know if he was related to Hiram, founder of Willits City in Mendocino County.

In the Office of the Recorder of Sonoma County are two small books bound in much worn leather. They are known as the Books of Possessory Claims. All the entries are handwritten and in order of chronology, starting about 1853. The legalistic ritual is very similar for each entry: "Be It Known to All These Present" that the named individual is a citizen, a resident of the County of Sonoma, is now residing upon the land described and which he wishes to graze or cultivate for agricultural purposes. This is done in accordance with the California statute pertaining to the defense of possessory claims enacted in 1852. Practically all claims embraced the limit of 160 acres; and only one such claim was permitted to a citizen.

On the 24th day of February, 1859, came W. H. Willits to designate and record his land as follows: "Beginning at a big redwood tree (blazed) about 15 miles below Healdsburg on the northwest side of Russian River at the foot of a small mountain about opposite a redwood Canion called 'the Pocket' thence along the foot of said mountain one-half mile to a live oak tree (blazed) at

13

the foot of another mountain, thence west one-half mile to a little redwood tree (blazed) standing near the foot of a mountain on the bank of a creek, thence south one-half mile to a redwood tree (blazed) standing on the side of a mountain, thence east one-half mile over a little mountain to the place of beginning."

This was an unusually detailed description. But we ask again, where was he? Remember that the modern Pocket Canyon is south and east of the Russian River. The "little mountain" sounds suspiciously like Lone Mountain, and I am sure that it was.

We learn further that Mr. Willits entered the first claim upon the site of the Great Eastern Quicksilver Mine in 1863, and later became a director in its operation. There was eventually cut upon his land some 18 million feet of timber before the gentleman retired in comfort in 1884 to his fine home in Santa Rosa.

One of the most interesting jobs undertaken by W. H. Willits was that of official chainman on the rough land subdivision survey of 1866. Thomas Pippin was the axeman for the survey party.

Aside from the nominal wage, Willits had a more personal interest in where the section and quarter corners were located. His next step in permanently securing the original claim was the changing of the first land description to somewhat match the new official sectionizing. That was not always easy. But in this particular case it seems to have been. I have at hand a copy of a contract drawn on May 28, 1872, between Willits and the partners Heald and Guerne. Willits agreed to deliver four million board feet of peeled logs "from his claim, it being the Northeast quarter of Section 30, Township 8 North, Range 10 West." Yet, I am inclined to believe the original Willits claim was shifted a little to the west to match the official survey.

This Willit's claim represents the entire northern half of the bottom land between the summit of Lone Mountain and west to the base of Pool Ridge. The mouth of Forgotten Valley was precisely at the northwest corner of the 160 acre square. That particular canyon might well have been "the Canion called the Pocket." The current question is: By whom was it so known in year 1859? Possibly by the man named Fife who left a firm landmark in Fife Creek, but no written record known to me.

In passing, I must say that the name Forgotten Valley was

bestowed quite as recently as about 1925. I remember the canyon fondly as Old Man Roebeck's Place. I believe the handsome hermit with the long iron-gray beard was Swiss in origin. My father used to visit the friendly man and I trudged along most willingly. I cannot remember the subject of their quiet conversations except that we usually departed with a sample of his excellent homemade jelly. The most memorable aspect of these visits was my special protection during the journey from the outside fence, built of interlaced poles and willow branches, into the picturesque cabin. Mr. Roebeck would firmly grasp the horns of the most pugnacious billy among the flock of goats that wandered around and upon his little isolated castle. I always arrived and departed safely, but much impressed.

The next land claims in point of time were made in 1861. However, another interesting homestead claim not far away was recorded in 1859. This was done by Elijah K. Jenner on the 12th of December. He stated that he resided in either Bodega or Fort Ross township. The land he wished to claim was only 75 acres in size. It was "an island in the Russian River about a half mile from the mouth of the main channel."

I cannot help but wonder if Mr. Jenner, from his home on Penny Island, could look over on the south river bank and see the deteriorating farm buildings which had been constructed, owned and managed by Peter Kostromitinov. Less than two decades earlier, the eminent Mr. K. had been an important citizen in this most eastern outpost of His Imperial Russian Majesty, Czar Alexander.

At the southwest corner of the official township plat made for the area surrounding and north of present Guerneville is a drainage labeled Helm's Creek. This name was known to the few visitors of about 1866. Yet for the past century this stream has been called Hulbert Creek. One of its principal upper drainages is called Mission Canyon for no reason known to me. A railroad was built into this canyon complex when Guerne and Murphy logged it in the years around 1885. The "dinky" and the "coffee grinder" locomotives hauled logs on flat cars up to the big sawmill in town. Although the dates will hardly stretch, I am positive that I saw and heard the old coffee grinder coming around the Ferngrove bend.

The surname of Shelby W. Helm unquestionably replaced some Indian name for the delightful stream which meets the river just upstream from old Guernewood Park. How he and Hulbert came to make a property exchange is no longer known. It does not matter. This business of sales and exchanges of real property before and after official claims were filed makes it impossible to even guess at many original land holdings.

At any rate, Shelby Helm did, on April 11, 1861, appear before the County Recorder and swear that he was resident upon "the north side of the Russian River one mile below the Pocket Creek." It would appear that this square 160 acres included both banks of the new Helm Creek upstream from where it entered the river.

Soon thereafter Henry Hulbert (whose name is so often misspelled Hurlbet) must have settled upon the land. Apparently, Hulbert must have been persuaded by Tom Heald and George Guerne to formally claim and pay up by pre-emption, on January 10, 1868, for three adjacent 40 acre parcels. A settler's pre-emption claim was supposed to be filed anyway, after the land was officially sectionized. Since the creek name was changed, and with only the meager land description, we must assume that Helm's land had been taken over by Hulbert in some manner.

In general, this area embraced Guernewood Heights and Park and across the river to run up Neeley's Hill. An interesting aspect of the situation was Hulbert's deed to the lumber operators being dated prior to confirmation of his grant. But Hulbert was well paid for his land, and his claim was undoubtedly legitimate.

Robert Barton Lunsford seldom used his given names. I know little about him except that he came west from North Carolina in 1854. He purchased a lot in '57 when Harmon Heald subdivided his city of Healdsburg. He was very active in buying and selling property in Guerneville town and vicinity through the 1870's and 80's. He also operated lumber and shingle mills at several places and with several partners. Lunsford cut the timber that stood on the town site proper. Richard Lewis and a man named Ely worked with him. In fact, Lewis (great grandfather of James K. Neeley) is often listed as a co-founder of the community. One reference source states that George Guerne himself said the town should have been named for Lunsford.

Lunsford was also said to have operated a saloon, but I found no written record of it. He also was said to have been a money changer and lender. That is quite logical. There was no bank in town until Wells Fargo and Company offered some service in that direction. In the rare county directories I find Lunsford dealing in lumber, but owning only small acreage as late as 1884. No record of his retirement or death is known to me.

Why he was said to have settled in May of 1860 I do not know. His claim was filed on March 28, 1861. He deposed that he was then settled upon land either in Salt Point or Mendocino township, "beginning at a redwood tree at the foot of a hill about twenty steps from the Russian River and about 100 yards below where two creeks empty into said river, thence following the meanderings of said river upstream about 600 yards in a direction 16½ degrees north of east to a stake, thence north about 1100 yards to a small pepper wood tree standing near a clump of redwood trees, thence running west 600 yards to a redwood tree, thence south about 1100 yards to the place of beginning." Lunsford declared this was his pre-emption right, which is to say, he was already a resident upon the spot.

A parcel of land of that description could be set down at a dozen different places in Sonoma County. From the description one cannot even assume he was located on the north bank of the river. But his later dealings leave no doubt that he was in the Guerneville area. In fact, the two mentioned creeks are obviously Livreau and Fife creeks. In a later description of a land survey found in the Guerne notes, there is a survey tie to the "southeast corner of Lunsford's barn." That is sufficient evidence to indicate that Lunsford, the founder, actually settled and lived west of Fife Creek in the immediate vicinity of present Murphy Ranch and Surrey Inn.

It is quite probable that Richard E. Lewis came down from Healdsburg to the Big Bottom in the company of Robert Lunsford. Two weeks following Lunsford's official claim, Lewis entered his. This was on April 11, 1861. That was the day when the faraway capital of the young Nation was shocked to learn that Fort Sumter was under siege by rebel South Carolina forces.

17

The most fascinating descriptive words in the Lewis claim were these . . . "on the north side of the Russian River on the 'Fife Road' where said road crosses Russian River . . ."

On the official land plat of 1866, Fife Creek is labeled far up in present Armstrong Grove. Now in '61 we find his recognized road a couple of miles south, and presumably leading to a ford in the river. This route would then most logically lead a traveler or wagon into the Pocket Creek roadway, such as it was. Who was this man Fife? How long had he been here? What was he doing on this great land basin of huge trees and perpetual green twilight?

I find no record of Fife in early claims nor in any land dealing in the official records. Yet he must have preceded Lunsford, or even Willits upon the Big Bottom.

Lewis claimed a strip a quarter mile wide and a mile north and south, using the river as the southern side of his property. This included the present townsite and north, as I shall indicate more precisely in a moment. Another small item in his recorded description is of some interest. His northwest corner (presumably on the east slope of Lone Mountain near the present school) was a "large burnt redwood." Such a landmark on the Big Bottom must have been a victim of lightning.

A more important item was the declaration that this 160 acres had been surveyed by W. A. Eliason. How a person at that time became a professional public surveyor I do not know. Eliason shows up in other land surveys of the period. It would appear that Lewis and Lunsford (adjoining neighbors) wished to see no future quarrels about the claim boundaries which embraced the cream of the virgin redwood forest.

I find no record of Lewis as a working lumberman. But I did find a record of an important land sale. On August 6, 1873, Lewis sold to Lunsford 112 acres described generally as follows. The south side would extend from Mill Street and present Main (Railroad) eastward on Main to the present post office, that is, a quarter mile. With a strip this wide, move north three-quarters of a mile, to Laughlin Road. Such a parcel would include most of the present town and extend east and west from Lone Mountain to the big "French tree" on the hill, that is, Woodland Drive and Palo

Alto Avenue. This parcel of land and virgin timber was valued at the then significant sum of five thousand dollars.

In the county directory of 1889, the proprietors of the Great Eastern Quicksilver Mine are listed as Richard E. Lewis and Company. Cemetery records show that Mr. Lewis and his close family are buried at Healdsburg. He was born in 1829 and died in 1894.

Heald and Guerne logging operation, probably about 1875. Note "choppers" at left on springboard platform to get above butt swell of tree trunk. Note corrugated log skidway to facilitate movement of logs by oxen. (JPD photo)

Livreau and Ely sawmill, 1873. (JPD)

3

Bull Teams and Great Trees

THE easiest land route from Santa Rosa Valley to Guerneville was where the early county road and later State Highway was located. This was from Forestville (or Forrestville) west over the low divide into Pocket Canyon. It is well known that the railroad was most strongly attracted by the Korbel and Rio Nido area timber, and not just the idea of connecting a small town with the outer world.

Building and maintaining a railroad right of way along the bank of the river must have been difficult and expensive. It was not until after the railroad ceased operation in 1935 that a road was built over the old right of way along the river between Rio Nido and Korbel. In the 1920's a road parallel to the track had been constructed as far as Rio Nido from Guerneville. Prior to that time, a vehicle had to travel up the Mines Road about one and a half miles, then off into the short canyon right, over the sharp ridge and down into the westernmost canyon of the Rio Nido spider web. This short but narrow and twisted Canyon Seven road must have thrilled many a summer visitor.

The easiest way into Guerneville by wagon was the easiest way out. This fact bore heavily upon anyone trying to cut lumber and get it to market. A note left by Julia Guerne would appear to bear this out. She wrote: "The first sawmill was operated by Joseph Lorm Sedgley about 1861-62 on government land." This mill was located a couple of hundred yards from the Olive Mill in Pocket Canyon. Later this structure became known as Santanella Winery. It is two miles from Guerneville. A man named Powers built a sawmill in 1862 near the Lewis Ridenhour place on the north side of the river. Sedgley was later a stage driver from Sebastapol to Bodega and up the coast beyond Point Arena. His stage was twice held up and robbed. Julia also noted the names Ballard, Russell and John Marshall Smith among the Pocket Canyon pioneers.

The late Nell (Smith) Morrill told me that her grandfather Torrence from Missouri, with Henry Beaver of Virginia were the first settlers down Pocket Creek. They felled big trees to get their ox teams as far as the somewhat open space on the "south side"

21

across from later Guerneville. The latter place was a dark wilderness of great virgin redwoods. But the new settlers did build a raft to take stock across the river to browse the forest understory. They were not interested in lumber.

I am a little confused with three Torrence first names. In 1864 two land claims were made, probably by sons of grandfather Shubael Hibbord Torrence, covering large parcels of Neeley Ridge and lower Pocket Creek. These original ownerships had long since been disposed of before my birth in the near vicinity.

One of the few names of the entire region which I cannot trace to any known origin is Mayes Canyon. Even the spelling is uncertain. I wonder if there might have been a female member of the Torrence family named May whose given name was thus commemorated.

Mrs. John W. Bagley, in her correspondence with a Healdsburg paper, declared that her husband brought the first milling equipment into the Big Bottom of Guerneville. This he did in August of 1865. It was necessary to build a road to the chosen site. I would guess that Lunsford made a deal with four partners to provide timber from his claim. I doubt if George Guerne ever engaged in cutting timber that did not come into his possession by clearly legitimate means. There must have been open temptation to do otherwise at this place and time. The official land survey was a year in the future, and the government had little means of preventing wholesale trespass.

The sawmill partners were Bagley, Tom Heald (brother of Healdsburg founder Harman, and also Guerne's brother-in-law), W. H. Willits and George Emile Guerne.

Bagley sawed the first board with the little steam driven saw, as he did the last board thirty-five years later. Both Willits and Bagley soon dropped out of this original sawmill partnership. In 1879 Heald sold his interest to Thomas J. Ludwig. In March of 1880, Rufus Murphy bought into the partnership. It was dissolved in September, to become Guerne and Murphy. This endured until 1892 when the Sonoma Lumber Company of Westover brothers and Robert Dollar bought the concern. George Guerne retired.

"D. L." Westover became an important citizen of the town and a resident of the old French home on the hill.

John Washington Bagley became the first postmaster when that office was created in 1870. That year the town's common name of Stumptown was officially changed to Guerneville. Bagley operated a general store. He was the community bone setter, tooth puller and first aid authority as well as undertaker and sexton. For thirteen years he was a school trustee. Somehow he qualified himself as a civil engineer, and his local land surveys were never questioned.*

As I have indicated, George Guerne was respected and admired in the town of my youth. I remember him well as a short, rotund individual with rosy cheeks. Leather puttees or boots and a slouchy dark felt hat with his business suit seemed to be his regular costume. I remember how he would emerge from the bank on Main Street at the southwest corner of the Odd Fellows Building, probably after a director's meeting. His horse, Faithful Fenita, would have been browsing at the grass on either side of the street as she pleased. Mr. Guerne would look up and down the street and then whistle shrilly for her. She would trot up with the light spring wagon for him to climb aboard.

George Guerne, not unlike some other lumbermen, must have suffered a twinge of conscience with the knowledge that this great virgin forest, possibly the most voluminous on earth, was being eliminated at his hand. He was serious about disposing of the Guernewood area as a public park at a much lesser profit to himself. He traveled to Sacramento and he engaged in heated newspaper debate with opponents around 1909 on behalf of making Armstrong Woods a State Park. Yet, I must make the personal observation that he might have emulated the philanthropist Colonel James Armstrong to the extent of donating a town lot or

---

*Bagley is credited in the State Board of Forestry Report of 1886 as the contributor of an amazing statistic. He reported that the trees from one measured acre on the Big Bottom produced 1,431,530 board feet of redwood lumber. Only about one-fourth of the tree was utilized under the crude milling methods of the time. The talented and versatile J.W.B. could also charm away warts as one beneficiary, my brother Clarence, so often recounted to me.

John Washington Bagley
1827-1906

Mr. and Mrs. George E. Guerne and **Faithful Fenita.**

24

two for use as a public plaza. Of course, D. L. Westover could have made the same magnanimous gesture.

It is doubtful if anyone working in the great virgin forest that fed the "big mill" of Guerneville ever gave any serious consideration to the possibility or desirability of harvesting a second crop of lumber from this land. I cannot recollect such a thing being mentioned during my childhood. My father, the expert chopper and shingle sawyer, could not comprehend why or what I was doing when I enrolled as a college forestry student.

At any rate, came the day when the last practically available log was transported to the sawmill. The boilers were allowed to cool. No more would the mill whistle pierce the quietness of the little village. In the woods the brittle snap of the falling axes and the almost musical curses of the bull whackers were heard no more. A bustling era had come to an end.

Mrs. Eunice Bagley described the event for a Healdsburg newspaper:

> "The sawing of the last log took place on Saturday afternoon, February 2nd, 1901. By courtesy of the owners, Mr. J. W. Bagley was invited to cut the last board. And in the presence of a large number of our citizens the veteran sawyer grasped the levers and the deed was done. Of those who witnessed the cutting of the first board in what was termed the big mill, in 1868, four were present to see the same hand cut the last board, namely Mrs. Lydia Pool, Mr. and Mrs. T. C. Pippin and Oliver Wescott. Only one man employed by previous owners remained until now. He is Henry Klein the edgerman, the right man at the right place . . ."

The effort put forth during those 35 years of chopping and harvesting the big trees would have to be termed intensive in respect to the operational methods of the time. Cutting quite naturally progressed outward from the principal mills and in patches around small mills. Movement of heavy logs was a major problem. A dozen or more yoked oxen were capable of skidding

25

logs only short distances. Temporary logging railroads had to be built to reach the richest timber stands.*

As mentioned, there was no particular interest in a long time investment in forest regeneration. How could there have been when the virgin forest appeared to stretch out forever? And naturally, there was little known, in a scientific way, as to what would happen on the cut-over land, except that the redwood species was persistently trying to maintain itself by sucker sprouts around stumps. And, strangely, this obvious natural fact gave rise to one of the fallacious folk tales which so often develop among those who need only to look instead of merely repeating what they hear. I am sure that my father and his lumberjack companions would have stoutly maintained that redwood seeds were sterile. The truth is that healthy redwood seeds are full of life and abundantly productive.

And another fact was that the harvesting of large redwood trees by man and animal power was less destructive than that of steam and steel cable which followed. In short, there could have been a splendid regeneration of the forest around Guerneville if that had been deemed desirable. The only help nature would have required would have been protection from fire.

But what was desired, especially on the rich bottomland where the tallest trees had grown, was no trees and no stumps, but instead a full application of some form of agriculture. On the land where some hopeful rancher did not engage in fighting the natural return of the forest, that process was occurring in several "succession" steps or changes in the natural plant community.

First, there began to appear upon the scarred soil surface, small plants and vines and poison oak midst the stumps and residual debris. Then, in three to six years the soil and the shorter stumps would be hidden by brush species, such as manzanita and the several ceanothus species, dogwood and huckleberry. Mixed with

---

*One proposed railroad spur was to run from Guerneville north into Armstrong Grove. See "The Guerneville Branch" by Fred A. Stindt, an excellent history of the construction and operation of the Fulton and Guerneville Railroad as first printed in The Western Railroader, Vol. 19, No. 2; and separately in 1955. San Mateo.

this second crop of vegetation there would be seen the sprouting hardwoods, including tan oak, madrone and pepperwood (Umbellularia). Eventually, these hardwoods would begin to rise above the brush species. And if the particular site was moist enough to support high timber, a few dark tips of redwood and douglasfir would be rising with the hardwoods. Then in time, thirty or forty years, the coniferous forest would have grown high enough to dominate the forest land once more.

I think I became personally aware of these changes when it was noticeable that the huckleberry crops, once so common on our home ranch, had become greatly diminished. This occurred as the trees began to stretch upward and rob the lower vegetation of most of the life-giving sunlight and, no doubt, most of the available soil moisture also.

The second Guerne sawmill, constructed in 1868, and generally called "the big mill." It ceased operation in 1901.

Photo A: Looking north from the Fife Creek mill pond in 1875. (JPD)

Photograph A was taken by professional Joseph Downing in 1875. The late Will Cole told me that the man on the log was Nate Manning, a citizen of some interest of whom I shall say more later.

The camera was obviously placed part way up the jacob's ladder of the Guerne and Heald Mill. That was a chute or track by which logs were moved from the pond onto the carriage for sawing. The pond in this case is a rather surprisingly small expansion of Fife Creek. The camera is looking almost due north. The mountain profile in the center rear is quite recognizable as the eastward thrusting shoulder away from Pool Ridge, situated directly above the later home ranches of James Read Watson and John Strode.

To reconstruct the camera site one would have to clear away the new tree growth approximately between the present Safeway Store and the old Murphy residence (on Fife Creek between old Railroad Avenue and Old Main streets extended).

The hill at left is the base of Pool Ridge. Livreau Creek (often

28

mispelled) would meander south along that hillside beyond the structures. These two streams were in fact the remnant drainages of the old river when it made an ox-bow around the northward reaching Lone Mountain "peninsula". The ancient Fife Creek drainage then flowed north instead of south.

The *Healdsburg Flag* of 1872 advertised lumber for sale by Livreau and Ely at their mill a half mile from Guerneville. That mill must have been not far into the middle background of Photo A. Occasionally in my early youth I would hear references to the old racetrack "up at the Livreau". Joseph Livreau was born in Missouri in 1821. His younger partner, George Washington Ely, was also from Missouri.

When George Guerne had become moderately wealthy, and before he took his family to live in San Rafael and then Santa Rosa, he played with some very fine race horses at the small track he constructed at the site of old Livreau sawmill. By 1892, he and Rufus Murphy, A. McFadyen and T. J. Ludwig, all well fixed with Guerneville redwood income, were prominent in the Sonoma County Stock Breeder's Association, based at Santa Rosa.

The house at the left (Photo A) was the George Guerne residence. These were obviously crude, unpainted structures. The several roofs are made of barn shakes at least three feet in length. Actually, this was fine roofing material. The tighter, somewhat more elegant shingles were not yet in local production when these houses were built. Shingle making machinery was installed this year of 1875. In my childhood it seemed that any commentary regarding a shake roof brought out one declaration of quality. The elders used to say, "A shake roof won't leak with a hole you could throw a dog through." My earliest impression was that such an act would have been a bit silly to start with. It still is, come to think of it.

There are a few garden plots about the houses. Sucker growth around stumps would appear to be about six years old. This would indicate that the first logging was done here. And this place also must have been near Lunsford's house and barn.

Julia Guerne was born in the house at left in 1870. On the back of the photo she gave me is a list of nine Guerne children and the birthdates. Her notation indicates that Alfred, the third child, was the first born there, in 1867.

29

The eldest, Louis Henry, was born elsewhere in 1863. All who knew the gentle Lou Guerne regarded him warmly. He was a bachelor who spent most of his life around the town. He played cornet in the Guerneville band. Probably he felt some sense of personal failure as the eldest son of a very eminent father. On several occasions Lou said to me, "Buster, get out of this town and make something of yourself."

I am sure the house in the picture is on or very near the site of a later two storey Guerne residence that faced east instead of south. At the later time the main road downriver went west on Fourth Street and crossed Fife Creek. That stream crossing was near the house in the picture, above Manning's hat. There the road turned south and then west again around the Guerne home. During my youth the old residence was deserted and deteriorated. Ivy and rose vines crawled over fallen porches. The old structure has long since been removed.

About the boy on the log I know nothing this hundred years later. Perhaps he belonged to citizen Nathaniel Everett Manning who stands with the pike pole on the log. Manning must have enjoyed an education considerably better than the average of his work associates. He enjoyed a better position than most as mill bookkeeper at the time the photo was taken.

Manning was born in Missouri in 1842 and came across the plains in '49. He attended what was said to have been the first school in the county, at Green Valley. He added to his education at Santa Rosa and earned a teachers certificate. After a little teaching and no success in business or at the Virginia City Mines he ran for county recorder on the temperance ticket. Naturally, he was beaten. He came to Guerneville in October of 1871 and went to work for Heald and Guerne. He was prominent in lodge work. From 1884 to 1890 I find Manning was the railroad agent. At one time he was a justice of the peace. I am not sure if he gave his name to Manning Flat on East Austin Creek.

It should be noted in passing that the Temperance Society was an active force in that day. Representatives sometimes held important gatherings in Old Stumptown which became Guerneville. For teamsters, loggers and millmen who lived and labored at a social level not much more enviable than that of their beasts of burden, the solace of strong drink and the companionship of the several saloons was an important source of relaxation. Most devoted imbibers ridiculed the temperance people. The Santa Rosa weekly *Sonoma Democrat* for late 1880 and early '81 contains several references to the violation of the saloon "Sunday Closing Law" in Guerneville. It appears that one case at law exonerated the saloon keeper who kept the "club house" open while he declined to release the Demon Rum.

As to the town itself, in 1874 there was a recorded population of 205 persons, only 62 of whom were female. These figures are indicative of an undeveloped lumber town. When settlers could go out upon the logged over areas to engage in their struggle of converting natural timber land to agriculture, the population would begin to grow and become more stable. Yet the town boasted a good hotel, two general stores and one saloon in 1874. There was an official U.S. post office in town. Thrice weekly the Clark Stage Line sent good quality passenger stages into the village from Santa Rosa, and returned them the same day. The route lay by way of

The mule team pictured here was on the summer bridge across the Russian River. Prior to the construction of the railroad in 1877 such teams hauled great quantities of lumber into the Santa Rosa Valley. It was said that during the height of the logging season all of the departing freight wagons would have stretched out a mile in length.

Forrestville, which is to say, down Pocket Canyon. Forestville (as now spelled) was founded by Andrew Jackson Forrester of Illinois in 1853. At any rate, the Stage Line advertised that its "Stock is good; the drivers trusty and experienced." It is interesting to note that schedules for leaving and arriving at Santa Rosa did not list journey time, but assured that a meeting would be made with steam trains from and to the town of Healdsburg.

John Folk's Hotel on old Main Street in 1878. The building was destroyed in the fire of 1883. The Clark Line stage is apparently ready to depart for Santa Rosa.

Looking east up Old Main Street from the mill, 1873. (JPD)

Photo Na: Looking southwest from lower slope of "the hill" in 1875. Probably the only defined street at this date was Old Main. (JPD)

The Henry Willits residence on Old Main Street, 1875. (JPD)

Southwest part of town in 1873. Photo taken from near present Armstrong Woods Road and Third Street. Note tram rails in foreground, no doubt for hauling logs at this date. Note men on stump in center foreground. Sawmill is at right middle distance. (JPD)

Photo P: Looking eastward over Guerneville in 1882. (JPD)

Photo P was taken in June of 1882. It looks east and a little north. The white French house is in the upper center, on "the hill." The "N" photos were taken near the house and they look in the precise opposite direction. Any present day attempt to duplicate Photo P would meet with difficulty. The camera site is covered with forest growth, and there are trees hiding the new town.

In the far upper right the smoke of a sawmill across the river makes a smudge. There must have been a low summer bridge in that vicinity, but it is not discernable. Moving left, the bell tower of the new school house is visible. Lower Old Main Street runs toward the camera and ends at the big mill.

Fife Creek is this side of the mill, and the railroad trestle crossing it is just left of the photo center. At the lower left is a plowed patch about the stumps. Just beyond is Livreau Creek, crossed by a wagon bridge and the logging railroad. Up the road, between the two creeks there appears to be an orchard. Somewhere in the left center of the picture was the chair factory of Marshall Florence. Very substantial kitchen chairs with woven rawhide bottoms were a proud product of this town.

The French house must have been built in the late 1870's by John Henry French. Several of his children were born there. The date of 1881 is set positively for the birth of son Percy Enoch, in whose memory a State Redwood Grove has been dedicated in Humboldt County. Our family lived there for a short time soon after the great earthquake while our new home down the hill was being constructed. My sister was born there then, and I maintain a faint recollection of the event. Whether this house was built prior to the house in which I was born in Mayes Canyon I do not know. Both have been occupied for an approximate century.

The D. L. Westover family resided on the hill for years, and he planted trees of many species there, and around the old mill site down town. The Guy F. Laws family acquired the house in 1913 and have continuously resided there.

Presumably French planted the vineyard below the house on the south and west slope. In my childhood the vineyard was neglected and barren.

Riverside Avenue bears upward to the right through the vineyard. I can't remember that name, nor any other applied to that road, and I have traversed it on foot a thousand times. Actually, we never walked on the roadway because a wooden walk two planks wide paralleled the clay road on the south side.

Down the hill to the left of the French house is another road winding up the hill. Near the first bend is a white house, unknown to me. It's place became the site of the Catholic Church.* Beyond that house the modest Clar residence was built about year 1907. I feel sure that this small opening in the high timber had been an Indian encampment.

The road proceeded up to the cemetery flat seen in the upper left of the picture. Shortly before the construction of French house it was intended that the cemetery be built where the house stands. Three bodies were indeed buried there. But they were soon removed to the present site farther up the hill.

The old Mines Road can be seen bearing off across the middle left of the picture. Near where that road and the hill road converge

---

*The building of that church in 1905 is described by Sonia Krivenko in "St. Elizabeth's of Guerneville," in the Mendocino Robin of June 1967. Ukiah.

is a white building. In that vicinity (now Fourth Street and Armstrong Woods Road) was the Lunsford shingle mill, and later the John Coon residence.

I don't know by what transaction Lunsford transferred the hill timber to John French, but the latter (and probably a partner named McFadyen) logged and milled the big trees there in the 1870's and '80's.

This brings us to the large redwood tree at the same level as the French house, to the left, midway between the house and the fuzzy tree top relatively near the camera. This big tree still stands on the property of Frances Perdue, which was the home of the large Smith family before and during my generation.

We called the old grandfather redwood the "hawk tree" for no particular reason. At least, there is no recollection of hawks nesting there. I played around the base of the old tree throughout my boyhood. I once rode a bicycle up the hill to its base; a feat not duplicated before or since, to my knowledge. Yet the greatest all-enveloping pleasure I think I have ever enjoyed occurred in its shadow while I had no concern for the great tree.

An older brother had walked me up the hill (there were very few houses on the hill then) to the Beatty home across the road from the tree. Someone created a small puddle of water in the meager garden in the front yard in which Willie and I could play. It was no larger than a dishpan. Yet it was a glorious ocean for the rose petal ships we blew across its surface. Captain Willie and I were probably in our fourth year of adventurous life on that day of innocent joy so long ago.

Why was this large, apparently straight-grained tree not felled and sawed into lumber? I have often wondered. Lately I learned that a clause in the earliest deeds provided that the land purchaser "distinctly understood" that said purchaser "does not have the right to cut or destroy a large redwood tree, a landmark . . . ."

There is a recent legend about this having been a residual spar pole left after other trees were felled. I don't believe that, for the simple reason that oxen and not high lead cables were used to move logs toward the mill at the time. My opinion is that this tree was precisely on the property line of the Lewis-Lunsford transaction of 1873 and others later. Technically, a tree growing on two properties is not to be cut.

Lastly, it should be noted that this tree (unintentionally, no doubt) would have marked the eastern limit of the proposed Lunsford Street on the town plat of 1879.

The author standing beside the "big tree on the hill" in 1973. A century earlier John French had declared the tree to be a permanent landmark. The author's father told of the time a lightning storm blasted part of the top off and the townspeople gathered five washtubs of wild bee honey from the tree remnant on the ground.

4

A Quarter Century of Settlement

DURING the dry summer and autumn of 1887 many destructive wildfires ran through the canyons of the Russian River Country. There had been heavy property losses in scattered woods operations and around the newly created farms. Volunteers worked desperately to stop the fires, but they were few in number and their efforts were without direction. Not until November rains started falling could the men return to their homes and jobs.

By this year, most of the large trees on the famous Big Bottom had been logged and milled. Chopping was in progress in Hulbert Canyon. George Guerne made an appeal to State officials in Sacramento to purchase and preserve his virgin forest at present Guernewood Park. There was little concern for public parks at that time, and he received no response. So logging began there in 1883. A few years later a new business venture of organized summer camping was introduced there.

Guerneville was yet very much a lumber town. The big mill would be in operation for another fifteen years. Small mills in the general vicinity chewed away at isolated stands of fine timber. And "split stuff," that is, posts, pickets, shakes, and railroad ties were important products. In fact, Guerneville at this time ranked second to Eureka as a lumber producing town. And it was the only genuine village in Redwood Township.

For ten years this town had been the terminus of the Fulton and Guerneville Branch Railroad, and it would so remain for ten years more. My mind retains a clear memory of the old locomotive turntable, approximately where Mill Street met Railroad Avenue. Probably it was seldom used to turn locomotives by the time I became aware of it. Since the bearing wheels had to be set below the track grade, a little round turntable pond must have existed all year, primarily as a mosquito breeder. At any rate, I associate the old turntable with water.

The hard working Italian immigrants had not yet arrived in any great number. The largest foreign immigration was undoubtedly represented by hardy, timber-wise Canadians from one particular area. Such names as Wescott, Banks, Ellison, Starrett, King,

Tomlinson, Campbell, Coulter, and Thrasher will be found in the records then, and some to this day.

In Guerneville in the mid-1880's the J. W. Morey Post, Number 81, of the Grand Army of the Republic listed 22 Civil War veterans in their sturdy middle years. Their war service represented the Union, from Maine to California. Probably the only Confederate veteran in the community was Theodon Yerger, the tailor. But he probably arrived in this town somewhat later. His shop was about where the Connell livery stable stood. In my time it was next to the shoe repair shop of the club-footed John Coll, an immigrant from Belgium, as I remember. It was not long before the German name Yerger was twisted into Yeager in our town.

There was gossip about bounty jumping and riding with the James Boys, but tailor Yeager told no tales and quietly plied his thread and reared several children, including son Bill who became a prominent sports writer in San Francisco. My brother George tells of his small urchin gang trying to irritate the old man one day. In response the tailor spoke quietly and said, "Do you boys like to shoot guns?" Oh yes, of course. So he belted on two holsters of horse pistols, and led the urchin parade to the river bank at the rear of the shop. There Old Man Yeager drew the two weapons and sent two condensed milk cans spinning down the sandy beach, both hands blazing. No small boys bothered the old gentleman thereafter.

Soon after the large trees were removed from the Guerne property on the flat south and west of Lone Mountain, hops were planted. I would assume that they were grown and harvested through the period 1890-1910. We have a family photograph taken there about 1899 at a tent camp. For good reason I was not present. But an older sister was sitting on my mother's lap. It was claimed that contaminated water at the camp caused her death a few weeks later.

My single remembrance of the hop field must have been dated about 1909. That memory impression was firmly registered out of the hullabaloo generated by the very small Margaret Coon. In spite of her youth she yet remembers having said to the bee on her sandwich, "I am going to eat you." Presumably she did just that, but not without being stung on her tongue.

These meager statistics seem to point to the hazards of the hop fields for young children. Nevertheless, it was common practice for entire local families to work in the fields at harvest time, especially when prunes, grapes and hops were gathered. It is important to remember that Guerneville could have become just another abandoned lumber town without some economic sustenance such as local agriculture and summer recreation.

Hop pickers and "low pole" hops at the south end of Lone Mountain at the close of the century. Snapshots from the album of Julia Guerne.

Photo B: Looking west down Old Main Street on December 11, 1887.

When the late Julia Guerne, who was born beside Fife Creek in 1870, gave me Photo B, she noted only that it was taken in 1887. The location of the camera is quite obvious. But there are some peculiarities about this picture that should alert any small town boy.

This was an unusually large gathering for a town of about 600 population. Citizens must have come together for some particular event, such as a political debate or patriotic ceremony. The men, and even boys, are attired in their "good suits". It must have been Sunday or a special holiday. Women and children in the wagon down Main Street appear to have tarried there, instead of at the hitch rack off to the left. At least, that's where the public hitch rack was during my childhood.

The "parking" facility was an important element in every small town along with the water trough. Our rack consisted of a row of heavy redwood posts set out from the schoolyard fence so that an unpaved sidewalk extended on beyond the weeping willow tree seen behind the Livery sign. A heavy iron link chain passed through center holes in the posts throughout the length of the rack. The original posts had been sawed from fine-grain redwood and were at least 12 inches square. I say original because generations of standing horses had chewed the corners and tops off the posts. And generations of school boys had so often "skinned the cat" over the chains that the heavy metal had cut its way deep into the soft grained posts.

Eventually early vintage automobiles could be seen nuzzled up against the hitch rack along with the horses. I distinctly remember one horseless carriage with wagon type wheels, except that it boasted a thin hard rubber rim instead of steel. It was steered with a horizontal rod across the lap of the driver instead of a wheel.

Before we leave the hitch rack, my conscience, quite belatedly it is true, forces me to comment upon a small prank of nearly three score years past. For any citizen who happened to have been attending an evening entertainment up in the Odd Fellows Hall, and who thereafter departed the affair to secure his wagon and drive home, and who found wagon wheel wired to wagon wheel along the whole hitch rack — I have this message. I don't know anything about it. Ask Andy Strode.

And that quite logically leads to the small boys in the picture. I count nine of them in the foreground, where small boys are inevitably found. But the most unusual aspect of this picture is not men or boys. It is the four visible dogs, all on leashes.

Dogs, chickens, and the most durable of cats enjoyed the free run of this town. The one somewhat domesticated animal that failed to bask in the warmth of universal human love was Cap Wendt's monkey. The creature dominated the white flag pole in front of the Louvre Saloon where Cap presided behind the bar. No one transgressed upon his domain and certainly not small boys. And woe unto the flowery decorations on any woman's sweeping "picture" hat that might go floating along on the street below. Of course, that nasty little monster appeared some 20 years after the dogs in the photograph had departed.

Some respected authority on that day in 1887 had unquestionably demanded that the dogs be kept leashed and out of mischief. There must have been a reason.

The nearest two-story building (right) was a Hall according to the sign. But the last Odd Fellows Hall, built following the fire of '94, was on the precise spot of the more distant and larger building in the picture. At the corner at the near right of the photo is a barber shop. The wall sign appears to read: "Shave 15 cents, Haircut 25 cents." Later a Rochdale Store (which might have been Cap McPeak's Grocery), then Drake's Butcher Shop, and eventually a pharmacy occupied this corner store.

At the time of the photograph it is probable that John Taggart's Guerneville Hotel was situated beyond the willow tree, and also the "Ice Cream Saloon," that is, if they were not totally destroyed in the fire of '83. To the right of the wagon, a sign indicates Harms Saloon which was destined to be destroyed by fire in 1889.

The tall man directly under the I in LIVERY died before I was born, but I am positive that this was Napoleon Bonaparte "Dinky" Turner, grocer and timber broker. His son and grandson of my acquaintance were cast in the same lean, long mold. The drinking emporium behind him was probably known as Thompson's Saloon. Connell's Stable is at extreme left. Ellison's Livery was down the street farther.

What time of year was the photograph taken? Certainly not in warm weather, as indicated by the clothing and overcast sky. It seems remarkable at this present time that every head then was covered by a hat, including the boys, girls and women.

Curiosity as to the reason for this gathering, and especially the leashed dogs, drove me to old newspaper files. I began with fall issues of 1887 because of the overcast sky. I am sure that the mystery was solved in the December 17 issue of the weekly *Sonoma Democrat* with the following article:

> Sunday [Dec 11] was a great day in Guerneville. A vast concourse of people gathered on Main Street to witness the imposing spectacle of a ballon ascension. Prof. E. W. Smith constructed the magnificent air-ship and inflated it with hot air. It rose majestically to the altitude of a mile, took a circle around above the town and then sailed slowly away to the southwest until it was lost to view in the distance. The inevitable photographer was around, and "took" the crowd, balloon and all.

If one accepts this solution to the Mystery of the Main Street Crowd of 1887, let the imagination dally over the small pile of street debris in the front center of the old picture. Could this not

44

be evidence of a fire kindled on the launching pad of Professor Smith's magnificent air-ship?

The tumbled topography and dense vegetation of most of the Russian River country along its last tortuous path west from the Santa Rosa Valley is hardly inviting to most types of aircraft.

It should be noted that Professor Smith used good judgment in two respects. He entertained the multitude in December when there was no serious chance of setting fire to the mountains. He also stayed on the ground while the balloon rose majestically. I read a newspaper account of another daring professor who rode his hot air-ship into the wild blue direction of Hood Mountain. This was during a Fourth of July Celebration at Santa Rosa at an earlier date. Several days later the lost birdman was reported to be alive at an isolated ranch near Sonoma, even after the indignity of being shot at by bewildered, and probably frightened, homesteaders along his unguided course of travel.

To my knowledge, only one passenger-carrying aircraft ever used Guerneville as a point of landing and take-off. The year was about 1920. I took Photograph H, showing the little World War One Curtiss Jenny, with my Brownie Number 2 Kodak. That camera was the poor man's "flivver" of the developing world of

Photo H: Hunt's Curtiss Jenny in Guerne's field about 1920. Note hop kiln beyond plane's tail.

popular photography, just as the Model T Ford was made available to the less-than-affluent citizen of a new cultural era.

And now, across the land, a handful of daring, or foolhardy, aviators were popularizing the new era of flight. The owner of this plane was named Hunt. He used the only open and relatively level field of any dimension in the entire vicinity. This was Guerne's field, upon which some 40 years earlier the world's tallest, most voluminous growth of redwood trees had stood in their pristine glory.

Note directly over the plane's tail the vague outline of the hop kiln at the south end of Lone Mountain. No hops had been harvested here for years. The land was currently used for dairy pasture.

Aviator Hunt and his plane perished in a crash at Napa some months after this picture was taken. But while he was at Guerneville he gave a number of daring citizens their first bird's-eye view of their homeland at five dollars per flight. My own curiosity and zest for adventure failed to overwhelm my inherent sense of discretion. And besides, five bucks was a modest fortune.

Maintaining historical accuracy as well as proper decorum now burdens me. I must tell of the most celebrated flight of that time and place. This first requires a brief description of congenial citizen Benjamin Roberts. For Ben, Guerneville was truly the Center of the Universe. The war took him away to infantry training for a short time. And once he had traveled by train and ferry boat as far as the Market Street loop in front of the San Francisco Ferry Building. This was an awesome, noisy, and fearful place for any country boy, I will personally bear witness. Ben, often and willingly, described his trauma and behavior when he was thus confronted with this urban madness. Said Ben, "I looked up Market Street and there was more people than you could shake a stick at. I turned right around and climbed aboard the ferry boat to head for home."

Ben's appetites were simple except in one respect. He did not shun hard labor with the railroad section gang or around the livery stable. A sack of Bull Durham and a plug of Star chewing tobacco were shared when he had them, or mooched when his overalls

46

pockets were empty. He loved simple melodies with a passion. But all the great classics must have been noise to his ears.

On one occasion young Jack Hetzel, in the backroom of his father's tobacco store, was laboring mightily over the clarinet score of *Poet and Peasant* Overture. Jack was on his way to a successful career as a professional musician. His only auditor on this occasion was the gangly Ben Roberts. Jack finished the piece and sat panting from emotional and physical exhaustion.

"Jack," said Ben, "Jack, for God's sake, play us a tune."

In respect to Ben's principal appetite, it would be straining poetic license much too far to simply declare that he often looked upon the wine when it was red. Heavy red wine was a local product. And Ben demonstrated his admiration for all vintners by drinking any fermentation in any quantity available. Nor did he seem to care a whit if the potage was red or winelike. Yet one would do our hero's memory an injustice to brand him either a common drunk or an alcoholic. Ben and alcoholic liquor seemed to be logically associated and entwined. The Prohibition Law might have somewhat hindered this course of true love, but it could not prevail.

Ben's initiation into the fledgling brotherhood of birdmen did not come about because of his personal enthusiasm, nor even with his full and legal consent. In fact, he was so peacefully sedated by an over-generous ingestion of liquid pain remover that he was quite unaware that he had become a guest and patron in Mr. Hunt's magnificent Jenny. On such special occasions the guest was always treated to several aerobatic loops and dives.

The recounting of what had happened high above Guerne's field on that day was so polished and honed during the dreary winter evenings around the stove in the Louvre Saloon that I cannot begin to give it the literary perspective the story deserves. Too briefly and admittedly with some inaccuracy, I remember Ben declaring in essence: "I just opened my eyes and there was Gabe's Rock right straight over my head, and all the wind in Northern California was blowing right up my backside."

Gabe's Rock on Pool Ridge in profile against the western sky.

Gabe's Rock was something more than an isolated chunk of hard shale rock protruding from the top of a small peak at the south end of Pool Ridge. Positioned in profile against the sunset sky, about nine hundred feet above the Big Bottom, it constituted in fact the western bastion of our isolated, little community. For us the rock was a sort of spiritual anchor point, immune to the vicissitudes of time and human behavior.

I suppose the rightness of its being there had removed our curiosity as to how it had acquired a name sometime back in the beginning. At any rate, it was only recently I learned that a certain George Gabriel is therewith commemorated. Julia Guerne once mentioned an "Uncle Gabe," although I believe this man was in fact her cousin, and he worked for a time at the big sawmill. Whether he made claim to the peak, or once lived there, I do not know.

I remember quite vividly my first visit to the peak. The motherly Maggie Shoemake, widow of Omer, and neighbor of the Coon family, had conducted a picnic outing for a few of us youngsters one day. For us it was a long hard walk up the mountain and back. For Maggie I suppose it was somewhat of a returning home. She was a daughter in the pioneer John Pool family which had homesteaded farther north on the not very hospitable timbered ridge.

John Pool had been active in a small way in timber and land dealing according to the sparse records. He was long since dead by the time I began to catalogue names and personalities in the world about me. But Grandma Lydia Pool was yet with us. She seemed so quiet and small, and in appearance reflected so very little of her Indian ancestry.

Photo Nb: Looking southwest from near the French house in **1882**. Note new schoolhouse at center. Connell's livery is at left (east) end of Main Street and the Guerne mill at far right. Virgin timber across the river. But the south end of Pool Ridge above the river appears to be scarred by rail and wagon roads. (JPD)

Photo Nc: Looking southwest from the hill about 1885.

Photo Nc was taken from the French (Laws) house, looking southwest. In the left background is the river and the virgin timber of Neeley Hill. The time is definitely between 1882 and 1894, as dated by the school belfry and the first substantial church structure at right center. The fire of 1894 eliminated most of the structures visible here; but not Connell's Livery Stable at far left.

If Photo B is properly dated as 1887, then this picture was taken around 1885. Directly below the school belfry in this picture is a two storey building under construction. This was the completed "Hall" shown on the north side of Old Main Street in the 1887 picture.

Above the boy's hat and a little left can be seen the Joost Saloon (later Louvre) at the corner of Railroad and Cinnabar. Above that are two box cars in front of the original railroad depot. The smoke plume against the hill (center right) is rising from the "big mill." The center of town north of Old Railroad Avenue is dedicated to piles of lumber and "split stuff" ready for shipment. A white horse and wagon is seen at center right. Of most interest is the flatcar loaded with lumber at far right center of the picture. This was the end of the tramway which ran north from the mill, thence eastward approximately along present Third Street.

On the back of the original photo is the pale blue stamp of Andrew Price, a professional photographer of Healdsburg during the entire 1880's.

5
Fire and Flood
and Some Wayside Wandering

ONE of the most amazing habits of the human tribe in its domestic behavior is its disregard of the harsh lessons of natural catastrophe. Guerneville furnishes a good example on a relatively small scale.

Up to the time of my departure from the village, considerable respect was shown for the potential flood hazard. Substantial residences within the original townsite practically always had living quarters upstairs above any anticipated high water line. Then I began to note single-storey construction on well known flood benches.

There is nothing mysterious about the cause of the floods. Four feet of rainfall during a season in this vicinity would be near normal. I find that more than six feet of rain fell at Healdsburg during the winter of 1889-90. Naturally, the seasonal distribution of rain bears a strong relationship to the overflow of stream channels. And the latter topographic condition explains the high flood water levels of the lower Russian River. Pressing hillsides and the twisted channel constitute a true damming impediment to the excess rush of water.

Probably the earliest white settlers along the lower river learned very soon about the flood hazard. Most of them were land hungry immigrants hoping to find and claim a family homestead. The official notes of Seth Millington, U.S. Deputy Land Surveyor, are interesting in this respect. During the summer of 1866 he established official land sections and set corner posts in this area. Thereafter, land transactions were practically all identified as referring to portions of certain numbered square mile sections. When his course brought him to the Russian River, Millington noted that he measured to the "ordinary banks" of the river. And "there is Corn and Vegetables planted within the banks." At High Water the river banks are overflowed. He also wrote:

> This township is one of the roughest I have ever Surveyed being, except on the bottoms of the Russian River and the Creeks running into it One Succession of Hills and Ravines Verry Steep in some places . . .

The first occupation and settlement upon the particular land area is a fascinating aspect of human history. We are quite certain that most of the Indian encampments along this part of the river were seasonal rather than permanent. I have to presume that the very first of the white settlers who intended to cling to the river banks here had not preceded the government surveyor by more than one decade.

Mrs. Eunice Bagley in her writing of early Guerneville history stated: "The floods of March 1876, April 1880 and January 1881 demoralized the lumber yard and injured the machinery in the mill . . . ." Records also reveal that the winter of 1889-90 was very wet, as were the three winters from the fall of '92 to the spring of 1896. The S.F. *Chronicle* of January 23, 1895 stated:

> The worst trouble is reported at Guerneville, a little town on the Donahue road which was nearly wiped out by fire last fall. At noon today water from the Russian River had almost reached the depot. . . . By 2 o'clock all communication with the town by telephone and telegraph was cut off.

Every winter from 1901 to 1909 was unusually wet. In fact, in mid-January of the latter year it was necessary to suspend railroad travel to the Russian River area because of high water.

The two winters from late 1913 to early 1915 saw great floods. I remember distinctly the last moments of the Old Year 1914. My excuse for being out of bed was the "entertainment and dance" in full noisy sway in the "brick building." But I was down on the dark street in front of the Louvre Saloon, watching with a few of the elders. The slowly rising flood level had been moving westward down the railroad track, and eastward from where Fife Creek flowed in normal times. At midnight the flood tides joined, and Railroad Avenue technically became a water course. I do not know if that happened before, but it was close in 1895, as noted. Some of the more devastating floods which followed may have been that high.

The winter of 1920-21 brought a great flood. I remember how slowly the steam train (carrying us daily high school commuters) tested the bridges and embankments where the debris laden yellow waters swirled close. This was the winter that the Clar Ranch

52

suffered the loss of a rowboat and three of its six milk cows to the treacherous muddy flood water.

Guerneville was very vulnerable to fire damage. About the only favorable factor was probably never recognized. This was the usual high atmospheric humidity. The wooden structures were relatively cheap and flimsy. There were no building codes and no system of fire protection. Because dwellings and commercial buildings were much less complex then than their modern counterparts, they could be replaced quickly and at considerably less relative expense. For example, as stated elsewhere, there was once a time of no inside toilets or bathtubs.

It has been said that prior to Guerne and Murphy Lumber Company constructing a general water service in 1885, a man named J. H. Morrow delivered spring water to homes for 25 cents per barrel. The new water company drew from the Livreau Spring over against the base of Pool Ridge. Water quality was excellent.

At this point it is necessary to purge my soul of a childish indictment I once harbored against Citizen Charlie Bean. Charlie was the son of a couple of the earliest settlers in the big timber. He worked for George Guerne as resident manager for the residual properties as long as the "ranch" remained at the south end of Lone Mountain. I doubt if Charlie ever worked for another employer. For many years, Charlie and his spinster sister Rhoda lived on the hill just below the cemetery. I lived farther down the hill. At any rate, the picture of faithful employee and resident manager Charlie Bean, striding down the road, wrench in hand, is vivid in my memory.

Charlie walked with a decided limp long before his toil-worn body was racked by arthritis. Walking was the conventional mode of locomotion for all except the most aged and sickly in those days, and certainly if the distance did not exceed a couple of miles. Charlie was in a hurry in these particular mental pictures that I conjure up. There sat the small boy on the lowest of the log steps alongside the public road after the Methodist Church bell (the common alarm) had sounded the dread warning. And there came Charlie downhill almost at a run. In some manner the concept had been planted in my childish mind that Charlie and his wrench were on a diabolic mission.

53

The fact that Charlie went from home to home once a month with his long receipt book collecting water bills did no good for his anything but sparkling natural image; and now in time of dire community emergency Charlie was on his way to shut off valves and thus prevent the use of water by those thoughtless volunteer citizens who would be frantically throwing buckets of the precious stuff on to the flaming structures. At this late hour I can do no less than cry a public apology for the error of childhood misconception. Charlie was, of course, making sources of water available.

Small sawmills and individual houses were occasionally destroyed by fire, without leaving an imprint upon the sparse historical records. The first major fire of record occurred in the early morning hours of March 23, 1883. This fire started in a Chinese wash house adjoining Oscar Morrison's merchandise store. A brisk west wind (at that unusual hour) spread destruction rapidly. Folk's Hotel and Taggart's Hotel burned, as did all of the six stores along with Omer Shoemake's Saloon. The new school and the town's single church were not damaged. No one was seriously injured.

A quarter century later the "China House" referred to the barn-like, whitewashed structure east of Cinnabar Avenue about a quarter mile, close to the railroad track on the south side. The half-dozen male inhabitants of the place spent most of their days and nights inside, talking loudly in Cantonese as they washed and ironed the village laundry. I rather doubt that our family could afford even the coolie wage such work earned. Laundering and ironing was hard labor in those days of scrub board and flat iron. The shaved head, long queued Chinese, in their flimsy blouses and trousers and paper soled shoes were naturally bizarre and somewhat fearful creatures as viewed by the town youngsters. We stayed away from the China House and did not bother the inhabitants, under strict orders.

In this period of California history the Chinese immigrants were not happily received in any community. There were certainly cases of physical abuse perpetrated upon them by hoodlums, and unkind words by other white Californians. Yet I can remember only one instance of intended harassment in our town, and I was a

54

Morrison's Store on Main Street on July 3, 1882. Note the flags. The store was destroyed by fire in March of 1883. Note at left the post office, Wells Fargo and Dietz jewelry store. (JPD)

personal witness.

Although I was quite young, the event was so shocking to my retiring nature that I remember it vividly. I remember that my father was wearing a straw hat on his bald head, so it must have been summer. He was also wearing the honorary badge of SPCA. I am not sure what authority this granted to him. But I feel that in that age of horsepower all the decency of any community would arise in wrath at an act of deliberate cruelty to horses. The particular incipient cruelty to which I refer developed when a pair of drunks stumbled out of the Louvre and spied several Chinamen (as we called them, without the slightest intent at racial derogation) walk-trotting toward the China House. The drunks shouted and each lunged for a queue to pull on. My gentle father lunged at the same time. I had heard something of his prowess as a boxer on the streets of San Francisco in his youth. This was the one and only exhibition of that skill I ever witnessed. The drunks must have thought they were attacked by a swarm of bees. They departed one way, and the Chinese another, leaving me and my spluttering father the sole proprietors of the field of combat.

About the time China House was deserted, Chinese laborers were brought to the village called Mercury at the Great Eastern Mine. The time must have been before and during the United States involvement in World War One, since quicksilver is an important war product. A number of the townsmen were also employed there. I suspect that the Chinese were all assigned to the digging labor described as mucking.*

An intelligent and congenial fellow known only as Jim was the general manager and counselor for the Chinese labor gang. He spoke English with little accent. Whether he was also the agent and advisor to six or eight Chinese operating a seasonal apple-drying plant up near Ole Hansen's place, I cannot say. I can place that approximate date because Frank Monticelli and I rode our bikes up there to sell them a wartime Red Cross membership. We failed; and I have wondered since if our brand of English was really as incomprehensible to them as their Cantonese was to us.

Mining and smelting quicksilver at that time, aside from the normal hazards of underground work, presented the additional hazard of salivation, or body poisoning from mercuric fumes. It was another tragedy that impressed me much more than that rather rare affliction. I had attended school with the two Snow children whose father was killed, with two other miners in the hoist, when the great earthquake of 1906 dislodged a rock in the shaft. It fell and crushed the ascending carriage. We children never spoke of that tragedy. But the accidental fall of the Faylor boy down into the water of the deep, dark and deserted shaft in 1918 naturally cast a long shadow over the whole community. He was nearly twelve years old, and I was several years older. What I remember well was probably the most impressive dream of my entire life. While the search for the lost child was still going on through the hills and woods around Mercury (and before a professional diver was brought to the old mine) I awoke one morning

---

See "Oh, Little Town of Mercury," by Sonia Krivenko in Mendocino Robin; late summer issue 1967. Ukiah.

almost violently. A male voice, which resembled no voice known to me at any time, had declared clearly and loudly, "The boy is dead."

Across the track from the China House was the calaboose. This one room, unpainted structure might have served as a substantial woodshed. A little light and air could enter only through the small barred window in the heavy door. Some scholar of Italian classics had daubed across the wall above the door: "All hope abandon, ye who enter here." Only an occasional obstreperous drunk was lodged in the city bastile, and then generally with the padlock open in the door hasp.

The next and last structure to be reached by road up the track toward Rio Nido at this date was Amos Alonzo Stagg's Riverside Resort and apple orchard.*

On February 20, 1889, the entire business section of town was wiped out. This fire started in the kitchen of the Grand Hotel. That place was consumed along with the Guerneville Hotel, post office, Wells Fargo Express, railroad depot, which then included the telephone office, both Connell's and Ellison's livery stable, and every saloon in town. The first permanent river bridge at Guerneville had been built by the county at the present location in early 1882. The north approach to the birdge was partially burned in this fire.

I remember holding my father's hand and walking across loose plant strips when the bridge floor was being reconstructed after another fire, perhaps a decade after the '89 fire. I am certain that the fear generated by the sight of flowing water sixty feet below the loose planking has haunted me many times since in troubled dreams.

The S.F. *Call* account of 1889 says in part:

> Frank Clar, bookkeeper for Guerne and Murphy lumber yard took the telephone out of the office and came out from town, attaching it to the main line, giving us all the news secured from there. He says nobody was injured and the loss is estimated at $75,000.

Uncle Frank had taught telegraphy at the prominent Pacific

I can find no relationship between our white bearded "Old Man Stagg" and the famous football coach of the same name. The Staggs were succeeded on this property by the Trospers and then the Jack Boschoff family of South African Boer origin.

57

Business College in San Francisco at an earlier date.

The most dreadful fire holocaust occurred on Saturday, August 25, 1894. It started from a kitchen stove in mid-day, and should have been promptly extinguished. But it was not. The fire eventually swept everything in the town proper, although Dave Connell's new livery stable was saved. The somewhat isolated school, the old sawmill, and the bridge were not damaged; but considerable piled lumber was burned.

The Guerneville and Western hotels were lost and the entire Odd Fellow's Block. This meant that the railroad depot and Wells Fargo office were again destroyed.

When a wall collapsed, the kindly country physician, Dr. J. A. Burns, and Oscar McKean were killed. Clyde Hewitt suffered a fractured skull. Ferguson, the local agent of Sunset Telephone Company, narrowly escaped death in the same incident.

Someone removed the one telephone from the depot and placed it in Connell's Stable. Later a lineman came and restored outside communication.

In Santa Rosa a very commendable effort was put forth by clergymen and other public figures to collect money, food and clothes for the destitute citizens of Guerneville. The County Board of Supervisors was clearly sympathetic but legally frustrated. No legal vehicle existed whereby they could officially render any material aid to this village of 600 souls. They did appeal to the U.S. Army and received the offer of twenty tents on loan. Forty years later, the interpretation of the Constitution's public welfare clause had been greatly expanded. County and city officials throughout the land did not hesitate to join with private charity in acting promptly to relieve the hunger of local victims of the Great Depression.

The next devastating fire broke out at midnight on March 12, 1906. The Grand Central Hotel was soon consumed and then seven other structures along the south side of Main Street toward the bridge. Someone telegraphed to Santa Rosa for help when the fire was discovered. A later message cancelled the request saying that by the time a train arrived with equipment the fire would have run its course. Very probably all mobile fire engines of Santa Rosa were horse drawn in 1906, and it is also likely they would not have found water to draw had they arrived in Guerneville.

The Joost and Starrett saloon in 1882 at the corner of former Cinnabar and Railroad avenues. This structure was destroyed in the fire of 1889, and its successor in 1894. When rebuilt after the fire of 1894 it was named the Louvre. The important town water trough was installed on the Cinnabar side of the corner. The false front was erected on the south instead of east side; the sidewalks were roofed.

At one brief moment (not recovered in any known document) badman Ab Garret stood with rifle in hand about where the camera was positioned and he shot to death a deputy sheriff seated on the porch who had come to town to arrest him. Ab then took off down the track to freedom until he was killed in Mendocino County. (JPD)

In this fire the Odd Fellow block on the north side of Main Street was severely scorched, but not destroyed. Quite accurately the *Call* reported: "Guerneville has had several bad fires in recent years and in each case the flames have had almost free sway."

Thirty-six days after that fire the great earthquake shook and terrorized coastal central California. Not only San Francisco, but cities on or near the fault from San Jose to Fort Bragg suffered great material loss and death of citizens. Santa Rosa was said to have been the most tragic victim.

Guerneville was well shaken. I have no recollection of the event, but my mother told me that she swooped me up and out of the old farm house. My older brothers considered it all great fun. Our father was working on building construction in San Francisco at the time. Eventually a message from him scribbled on butcher's paper was delivered by some traveler.

The death of three miners caused by a falling rock at the Great Eastern Mine is mentioned elsewhere. Dislocated news sources and newspapers make it virtually impossible to find a record of suffering and loss in small settlements. At Guerneville older brother George recollects men cleaning bricks that were shaken out of the walls of Odd Fellows Hall, for use in reconstruction. Tunstall's livery stable was practically demolished. Numerous residence chimneys were felled or twisted askew.

Earthquakes are undoubtedly the most terrifying of Nature's angry manifestations; not alone because of painful physical disruption but in the shattering of Man's only solid psychological firmament, his true Mother Earth.

The fire lessons of the past were not entirely ignored. A news item two and a half years following the earthquake tells of a report delivered to the fire commission, presumably a local unofficial association. Butcher A. P. Mosley reported that over one thousand dollars had been donated and several land sites promised for the hopeful construction of a 40,000 gallon water tank. Pipe lines were to be laid along the main streets for fire emergency. The capable Robert Noel Tunstall was president of the commission. Yet, to my knowledge, nothing came of this civic betterment proposal.

The scribing in the lower left of the Photograph C is difficult to read, but it says: "Guerneville Fire Sept. 25, 1919."

I remember the fire well. And I know why Newton Lark made the photograph. He was the local photographer as well as the town druggist. He was also a primary fire victim. He and his Uncle Fred Warne were associated in business at this time.

In addition to his commercial enterprise, Lark had in some manner acquired the dubious honor of becoming Fire Chief of Guerneville. In years past (and in some places up to the present day) recognized status on the community fire department often carried with it political and social prestige of considerable stature.

60

Photo C: Ruins of the fire of 1919. Odd Fellows Hall across old Railroad Avenue (now Main).

This could hardly be said of the volunteer group of citizens listed as the town firemen of that place and time. This is not to say that a tap of the Methodist Church bell out of scheduled hours of worship would fail to arouse the citizenry. Quite the contrary; every ambulatory citizen was immediately alert and ready to attack the Red Demon upon the sounding of the alarm. Their particular weakness was related only to too few drills, little organization and lack of funds for equipment.

The Santa Rosa *Press Democrat* did not heap honors upon the fire laddies and least of all upon Fire Chief Lark. Rightly or wrongly, he was said to have been the only possessor of knowledge about a certain pipe valve that when opened could have made available the water reserve in a high tank recently set upon a tower in Westover Park for that very purpose. I am inclined to question the accuracy of the newspaper statement. At least, I have no personal recollection of tank or valve. And a whole town can't hide such vital information from an active youth.

The underground pipe triggers a somewhat related memory. There was a legend of the great log which underlay the town. This was such a fleeting ghost of gossip that most urchins might not have possessed the degree of imagination necessary to store it away these three score years, as I have. At various times workmen in the ground, digging wells or cesspools, would tell of encountering a log, soggy but firm, the grain and alignment pointing in one direction. The town is situated upon or above what had been the river bed some thousands of years ago. Quite credibly, two or eight or ten thousand years ago a grandfather among the giant redwoods could have gone down to rest in the permanently wet soil. That's what the elders said.

Fire Chief Lark was not locally condemned for his alleged failure at the valve. The fact is that he was the recipient of many genuine expressions of sympathy when the smoke had cleared away. This was because the rubble in the immediate left foreground of the picture represents the residue of what had been the comfortable home of his family, consisting of wife and four children at that date.

The eldest child, seven year old Marion, had been a witness to suspicious activity at the time and place of the fire. And that essentially was the reason for the taking of the photograph. The picture was to be used as evidence in the trial of the People versus Hocker and Cannon on a charge of arson. The People in the shape of a formal jury refused to accept the testimony of the serious young lady. She declared, and the townspeople believed, she had seen from her sleeping porch the pickup truck of the partners who operated the dry goods store represented by the right, or western half of the rubble beyond the Lark home foundation. The time was approximately one o'clock in the morning of Thursday, September 25. At that hour in that month even a crowing rooster could have been heard throughout the sleeping village.

Hocker and Cannon, it became known during the trial, had been brought before a court in Arizona some years earlier on a charge of arson. I feel sure that my memory serves me correctly in this respect. For my own part, I can make a deposition only to the effect that I was personally irritated at the joviality expressed by one of the partners during the fire. And I was further irritated when the other chose to produce a graphaphone and play the old Spanish American War hit, "There'll be a Hot Time in the Old

Town Tonight."

Consumed in the blaze was the home rented by Reverend Dains. He was only a short time resident of the community, as were the partners Hocker and Cannon. The Dains' home stood at the left of the electric power pole (left) behind the Lark residence. Farther down Railroad Avenue to the right, or west, the Guy F. Laws billiard parlor and tobacco store was totally destroyed. (From 1913 to about 1916 the Laws' Ice Cream and billiard parlor had been across the street, at right edge of Photo C).

The heap of corrugated iron in the picture center had been a general store originally built and operated by Omer O. Cobb and later managed by his capable widow, Antoinette M. Cobb (mother of Anthony and Gertrude Lauteren (Johnson; Shulte)). At the date of the fire the eastern half of the store had been operated by Simon B. Buckner, selling groceries. I had worked for him that summer, about 12 hours daily for a wage of one dollar a day.

In the evenings I worked across the street at the River Theater. I was the film projectionist. The work day ended at about eleven o'clock or midnight there. I was not yet 16 years of age. Joe Buttner, a few months younger than I, was my assistant and then successor.

When my sophomore year of high school at Santa Rosa began, shortly before the fire, I left the grocery store job. The summer rush was over, of course, and store stocks were very much depleted. The newspaper stated that Hocker and Cannon lost stock valued at $19,000 which was insured for $14,000. It is most doubtful if that value of stock was on the shelves at that late date.

On the night of the 1919 fire I was alone, sleeping in the rear of the post office building, perhaps 200 feet right, down the street from the pile of rubble and just beyond the pool hall which burned. My mother had gone to San Francisco on post office business. I think someone yelled at me through the window. I roused myself enough to look out and see Carl Proschold up the power pole just off the picture to the right. Flames were crackling and throwing a weird light among the buildings. Carl was apparently cutting wires and yelling like a banshee. As I reconstruct the situation, it seems more peculiar than ever that I could have slept so soundly with practically the entire townsfolk up and

63

running about outside my window. Proschold was a friendly, noisy extrovert who was right in character up the pole and yelling orders. I cherish my recollections of him.*

After the ashes had cooled and the night's activity was being rehashed from every angle, I would hear such remarks behind my back as, "I hear Buster Clar said, 'Don't wake me up, it aint Christmas.' "

My mother had been postmistress for several years. We two lived in the rear of a rather ancient structure used as the post office. The remainder of the family was temporarily scattered. Probably my sister was attending boarding school in Santa Rosa. I am sure my mother felt that this cultural opportunity would help rub off a bit of the earthiness inherent in exposure to life in a summer resort town. I was up each school day morning ready to board the eastbound train for an hour's ride and then a mile walk to high school.

I had no concern whatever about the burning of government property. Most of it was just printed paper money and stamps regardless of what value the average private citizen might put on it. Instinct and training told me to leave it alone. And I soon found that I had to insist that volunteer firefighters do likewise. The difference between an allegation of looting as contrary to property preservation was naturally too subtle for well-meaning citizens to grasp in the heat of a general holocaust.

But personal property—now, that was something else. I took a quick inventory of our modest living quarters and made a thoroughly sound decision for a fifteen year old boy. I picked up my shotgun (inherited from my warrior brothers), climbed on my

---

*Probably this was both because of his Hail Fellow congeniality and my lifelong understanding that Carl had furnished the skin for a graft performed by his mother-in-law, Doc Cole. She was much respected, especially in the treatment of burns, in spite of general community doubt as to her technical qualification by medical school training. On the Fourth of July of my fifth year my cautious father took me to the center of the river bridge to explode three packs of firecrackers in safety. A spark entered my pocket and the resulting burn from groin to knee almost cost my right leg. The scar is precisely the size of my spread hand. Unquestionably, my father saved my leg by placing his hand inside my tough overalls to take the brunt of the exploding firecrackers.

bicycle (for the purchase of which I had saved my nickels during one and a half years of delivering city newspapers around town) and rode north to the wet pasture beyond Marshall's house. There I deposited my gun and bike in a clump of redwood suckers surrounding a large stump. That done I returned to the fiery front unburdened by personal problems.

I observed the last spasms of the fire mostly from the top of the post office structure. I remember three distinct blazes in the shingles while I was there. Some man was up there with me most of the time, actively helping and directing our mutual small battle. I remember only that he told me he was a member of the Oakland City Fire Department on vacation. I wish I could put his name on record.

Strangely, I can't remember if I climbed on the 7 o'clock train for school that morning. My mother must have returned as soon as possible. I remember her saying, "I was told you performed very well, son."

And so, as boys must, I grew up a little in the early hours of September 25th, 1919.

Exactly four years later, in September 1923, the town faced a threat of total devastation from a forest fire which jumped from one ridge top to another in great balls of fire, according to witnesses. I believe that was literally true. This was the day that Berkeley burned and more than 100 fires ran wild elsewhere throughout the State. Weather was extremely dry and windy. Miraculously, only a few structures around the town of Guerneville were destroyed. Railroad box cars and some unclean cattle cars were made available. Citizens loaded furniture and other property into them. The trains were ready to move in either direction as the fire dictated. I was busy enough in Berkeley that day. At home my sister found great amusement in the fact that our mother kept shooing away good neighbors who tried to move out her furniture. As a bride and as a young mother on a wooded hillside ranch during earlier years our mother was actually more of a hardy pioneer than she would have acknowledged. She was not about to be stampeded by another forest fire.

The 1923 fire did have one very beneficial effect. It convinced enough citizens that a responsible, legally organized, tax-funded

Guerneville Fire Department must be created. And it was.

On February 27, 1937, the stove used to heat the River Theater prior to an evening show apparently generated enough heat to ignite the stage area. Before the fire was extinguished a damage of $20,000 was incurred. Randall Starrett was fire chief at this time. His organized volunteer crew confined the fire to the theatre interior.

Soon after this the old Central Hotel was removed and The Grove Dance Hall was constructed there. My employment in the State Division of Forestry throughout the entire State did not permit my visiting the home town very often.

It is difficult still for me to accept the fact that on October 19, 1963, a fire, from what cause I do not know, completely destroyed The Grove and the Odd Fellows Building. Gone now is the "brick building" which for several generations of small boys was the biggest building in the world at the Center of the Universe.

In Photograph C the camera was looking southeast across Railroad or Second Avenue, presently known as Main Street. Rails are faintly visible beyond the rubble. In the far background, right of center, is Mayes Canyon across the river.

The River Theater and Meat Market, at center, occupy the site of the first railroad station and freight shed. In 1912 those depot facilities were moved to the right (west) a long block, and constructed on the north side of the track, as described in another photograph.

The near side of Railroad Avenue in the picture will first be discussed. This lot behind the camera had been part of the vacant ground in the center of town which served so long as the storage center for shipments of lumber and split wood products. Long ago the town baseball team used to play on this lot which was bounded by Railroad and Third, Cinnabar and Church streets. I do not remember that, but I do remember a small circus erecting tents here about 1909. The O. O. Cobb corrugated iron department store was the first structure in the central space, and that must have been built about 1907.

Left of center in Photo C is a white building with gable roof and false front. It faces the Theater, directly across Railroad Avenue.

This edifice housed the *Guerneville Times,* successor to the *Russian River Advertiser.* The dark shed at the rear housed the widowed editor. And the dark, gabled dog-house structure protruding from the west wall of the *Times* building is, if I do not err, nothing less than the town "firehouse."

In that open-ended, unpainted shed was a wheel cart supporting a reel of canvas fire hose. I hope I do no injustice to the town elders and volunteer firemen of that day, but I suspect there was no other equipment nor tool caches maintained specifically for fire protection.

For the moment let us consider the little four page newspaper which came off the ancient, flat-bed, hand rolled press each Friday. At about age twelve I spent some modestly productive hours around the shop as printer's devil, hopeful type sticker (compositor was the elegant term) and paper folder on press days. I can't remember any pay, but there may have been some.

This small experience in the world of the "ink stained wretches" actually gave me an appreciation of the art and craft of printing that has been of value throughout my life. From trying to set a "stick of type," and much worse, distributing the tiny individual monsters back into each home box, I learned to appreciate the dexterity and patience of so many thousands of printers over the centuries since Gutenberg. Fortunately, I learned early that monotonous or highly refined piece work was not for me. In fact, the only job I ever walked away from (without notice and with a sense of personal failure) was apple picking for Freed Hoffman. It was no matter of wage or physical effort; I simply failed to qualify in my own opinion. He never spoke to me about the event. But a dozen years later in a regular commentary he wrote for the *Times,* I was gratified to read that he commended my judgment in responding to my inherent temperamental lack of harmony with such work as apple picking.

Andy Smith was owner and editor of the *Times* at this period. He had retired after 40 years as press foreman of the S.F. *Call.* The short, round and gentle Albert Chaigneau, master of Ferngrove, was the nimble-fingered workhorse of the monotype boxes. I remember this kindly man most for the chicken sandwich he shared with me one lunch hour. His wife had prepared it with lettuce and mayonnaise and possibly other tasty things new to my tongue. That gustatory delight (and a sometime piece of Nell Smith's apple pie) have remained through the long years as heretofore unrecorded monuments to two housewives in some deep recess of my memory.

My father was a thoroughly decent man with little formal education. I believe the latter condition actually accounted for his having felt at home in this community. Yet he shunned the camaraderie of the saloon idlers. To him, the *Times* office represented the town's cultural center. He recommended that I spend my spare time there where I might benefit by listening to the conversation of a select few of the elders.

The fact that my father's judgment was wise reflects no credit on the community attitude toward the welfare of its youth. There was no boy scout or other program for boys except their own organization of baseball teams. Only the Beldens, Ralph and Pet, contributed substantial adult assistance toward the latter activity. There was no dearth of time-consuming activities for youth outside of work and school. Hunting, trapping, fishing and swimming were no farther away than the edge of town. But there was nothing resembling a public library, and no slightest indication of regret at such a lack that I can remember.

Perhaps that is why I appreciated the special concession on the part of Editor Smith that I be permitted to read the half dozen volumes of Horatio Alger that in some manner he had acquired for public sale. Very probably I was the only reader of those books.

I doubt if my youthful personality was modified either for better or worse by this experience. Author Horatio Alger had written a one-formula book for boys with fifty different covers and titles. The hero was a poor boy who worked hard to support his widowed mother. While he polished the boss' boots he learned how to go about cornering the world market on wheat and thus became a successful, happy millionaire, with no worry about the hindmost. Alger never attained financial success himself. But he reflected accurately the so-called protestant ethic of hard work and profit-making which dominated the nation's social and business morality, until brought into question by the violent cathartic of the Great Depression.

Of course, there were many fine books available for boys and girls if parents had been aware or felt they could afford them. One literary treasure our family acquired almost every Christmas was the English book *Chatterbox*. It is not likely that today's youth would be enthusiastic about such a stuffy compendium of short stories, pen sketches, poems, puzzles and what not. But then of course, we were true children of the Victorian Age in spite of our geographic and national heritage. "Dime Novels" were contraband, alleged to warp the moral fiber of any wayward child who read one under the bed covers. How innocuous would seem all the adventures of Frank Merriwell compared with present day evening television programs.

At the front corner of the Times Building a sort of arbor can be seen shading the fire house. This was the residue of a not very impressive Fountain. And the Fountain had had its origin in a dream of the Improvement Club. My mother was a teacher of piano and one of the cultural leaders of the community. I have been told that a person other than she had been delegated to negotiate with the heirs of Colonel James Armstrong, who then owned the property. The worthy goal was to create a town plaza here across from the railroad depot. The original project was diminished into a small drinking fountain fabricated of cobble-stones.

One good thing accomplished by the 1919 fire was a substantial widening of this street. It had been quite dangerous when trains were moving through. The rails were high in the unpaved street, and they could have trapped an auto or even a wagon. This was especially no place for skittish horses during train time. That is probably why the town hitch rack was located on Old Main Street a block away.

Those structures being rebuilt were set back to the present street alignment. About 1921, Mrs. Cobb built a modern type post office structure approximately across from the meat market. A cement pavement was also laid in front of the new store fronts. The earliest post office I remember was located midway in the brick building and opening on Old Main Street. In fact, I remember the time some obviously hungry safe crackers blew the door off Postmaster Tom Duncan's safe. That must have occurred about 1912.

The dark, two story building beyond the corrugated iron garage (far left in photo) was the Louvre Saloon Hotel or Annex. The rooms were originally built over a beer garden. That hotel was built essentially to meet a particular State law which prescribed that liquor could be sold only at hotels having a minimum number of bedrooms of a minimum specified size. This could have been around 1913. The National Volstead Act or so-called Prohibition Law was enacted at about the time of the 1919 fire.

I have a faint memory of seeing the redwood trees being planted in front of the beer garden. The only other memory I have of this Louvre Annex involves the ticket desk during some community dinner. There was congenial Joe Keaton, well primed for the festivities. Joe was balancing a five dollar gold piece on the tip of a finger, obviously trying to determine whether it was made of nickel or gold. Silver and gold were common tender then. Paper money was regarded with some suspicion, at least among country folk, until about the First World War. I remember my father bringing home three twenty dollar gold pieces as his earning for one month of hard work.

The "brick building" or Odd Fellow's Hall was, quite naturally, one of the most massive edifices in the world of certain small boys. It was built soon after the big fire of 1894. Masons, Druids and Eastern Star also used the lodge room facilities. Kitchen and lodge room occupied the entire south half of the second floor. Some public gatherings were held in the lodge room, possibly because it was small and more comfortable than the dance hall. This was a heavily carpeted and tapestried room. Small boys who had no business messing around had fun counting the black balls and white balls in a collection box which unquestionably played an important part in the social structure of the lodge community of that small town.

The north half of the second floor was primarily for dances and stage "entertainment." To the left (east) where windows are absent, was the stage. I first trod the boards there during a Christmas play when (unquestionably through my mother's influence) I starred as Santa Claus. My mother generally served as director, stage manager and general boss at such affairs. On this occasion of my show-stopping stage career I must have been eight or nine years old. How clearly do I remember that the show temporarily stopped due to the difficulty I had pushing a suffocating mask over my face and pushing my padded person plus knapsack out of a cardboard fireplace when the cue word sounded forth. I also remember that at least one prominent business man of a later era bawled that night in his father's arms at the sight of that peculiar midget St. Nicolas. I received a *Chatterbox* as a present from my family at that party. That was indeed an eventful evening.

The only entrance to the entire upper floor of the building was on Old Main Street at the southwest corner of the building. This was adjacent to the bank. For an enterprising youth, especially one lacking a ticket, it was no trick to shinny up a cast iron round porch pole. From the porch roof one could peer through one of the four windows directly into the dance hall and stage area.

The blurred sign on the high west wall of the brick building was not there when the world began. There was something else much more interesting. A rooster at least twelve feet high stood proudly in his "Can't Bust'em" Overalls. Under him was his declaration, "Something to Crow About."

I believe the Mercantile Company sign referred to Oscar Birkofer's general store, and not the earlier Rochdale Store, which was some type of chain institution. Before discussing that I have a comment about signs in general.

The common country fences were all made of driven pickets. Even barbed wire fences were rare. Picket fences were strengthened along the top with a running board of about one by eight inch dimension. These stringers furnished an ideal place to tack metal advertisements or political cards. There must have been numerous household and farm commodities named in such advertisements. But one above all others stands forth in my memory. This urged passers-by to "Use Queen Lily Soap." I presumed then, and still do, that this advice represented a most dubious honor paid to a well known lady then in retirement. She was the last reigning monarch of the Hawaiian Kingdom, Queen Liliuokalani.

Probably major industries took care of their own advertising. At any rate, large signboards were most uncommon. Sometimes one would be confronted with a large red bull painted on a flat wall.

71

Out of respect for Victorian sensibilities a pole fence was properly painted in the proper place, and underneath would be the words Bull Durham Cigarette Tobacco. Any wide barn roof with good roadside visibility was almost sure to boast a sign simply reminding travelers of Lydia Pinkham's Compounds or Dr. Pierce's Golden Medical Discovery.

Returning to Rochdale stores specifically, the first I remember was at the near end of the brick building. At that time, when the rooster crowed on the western hall, there was a vacant lot where the theater and butcher shop appear in Photo C. Occasional carnival shows would set up temporarily in this space, especially during the prevailing summer carnival atmosphere of this resort town. At a later date the Rochdale enterprise was moved to the far east end of this block.

For me a trip to the early store was high adventure. There was much less packaging of grocery products then. If a purchaser could afford it, flour and potatoes were acquired by 50 or 100 pound sacks, and bacon by whole sides. Of course, there was no refrigeration except ice boxes used by butchers and saloon keepers.

Kerosene was generally pumped by hand or drained from a barrel into the purchaser's half-gallon or gallon cans. Sometimes he ordered a square five gallon can. The important thing for a small boy was the nonchalent slapping by the clerk of a small potato over the end of the can spout as an improvised cork. By the time I became a grocery store clerk the sale of small quantities of coal oil (we rarely said kerosene) was rather uncommon. Nevertheless, I have often wondered since if some customers were not genuinely unhappy about the kerosene flavor that must have been incidentally acquired by hand-wrapped bread and other unprotected food commodities.

The big show for the small boy in Rochdale Store was action at the big red coffee grinder decorated with golden floral pieces. It was worth the price of a pound of coffee beans just to smell the rich odor and watch Sonny Peugh or one-armed Chris Baagoe (Bow-gie) crank the double wheeled grinder. Chris had lost an arm at a local sawmill in his youth. And I longed for the distant day when I myself would be able to throw a sack of flour on my shoulder as they did and walk out to the waiting wagon. The whole truth is that the white residue of flour on the shoulder demarked the nonchalant life of a merchant prince in the fascinating world of my childhood.

Various merchants came and went in the remainder of the lower floor of the brick building. There was the drug store. And there was the Capital Saloon of Pete McKenna. Dave Hetzel's tobacco store opened on the Main Street side. In the rear he rolled a fair grade of cigars from material he grew locally.

At an earlier date, before the removal of the train depot, Alec Walls' saloon was through the alley on Main Street. I was a very small boy when I first had a taste of whiskey. And it was at Alec's booze emporium.

Small boys and those habitual imbibers recorded on the local "black list" were not supposed to hang around saloons. Destitute wives and desperate mothers of that era could take the legal course of declaring that the Demon Rum was causing economic disaster in their homes because of the weakness of some particular sot. Said sot was thereupon blacklisted, and so far as I ever knew, refused service in all licensed bars. Few kids of my generation had any particular interest in liquor other than the one cent a flask bounty on empty whiskey flasks, commonly referred to as "dead soldiers."

As I remember my first and only binge in Alec's Saloon I was with my father and Uncle Frank. The latter had probably just stepped off the train at the Old depot. We were not drinking people. In fact I feel certain that we entered a quiet side room by way of the "Family Entrance" available to ladies and escorts.(I can't imagine any female person in front of or behind a bar in that day.)

I vaguely remember an animated conversation among the several men present, possibly a business conference. I was seated on my father's knee and enjoying the action. I do remember taking a sip out of the glass he held near my nose. Probably I was all of four years of age, but certainly no older. That was my downfall. The smell and taste of alcohol has been peculiarly repulsive to me ever since.

I believe it was the summer following the 1919 fire that I worked in Jack Starrett's butcher shop, shown in the picture. By that date Mr. Ford's "tin lizzie" had supplanted the light two-horse delivery teams. The great majority of tent camps and cottages were supplied with groceries, meat, and in later years, with small quantities of ice. What I remember best about the well-kept delivery horses was their response to the driver's foot brake. He could sit on the high seat indefinitely working over his order pad. But let his foot hit the brake pedal and both horses shot forward almost violently.

My primary duty as butcher's helper, along with Frank Monticelli, was making deliveries and taking orders. That routine in itself offered quite a widening experience for a sensitive country boy. At this time the Volstead Act was modifying the general mores of the Nation in a manner quite contrary to the intention of those people who had instigated this "experiment noble in nature."

I never had anything (well, practically not anything) to do with peddling or drinking bootleg liquor. And at this late date I certainly would make no insinuation that the numerous empty gallon jugs I picked up each day during meat delivery service had ever contained any kind of liquid, least of all the sour wine produced upon the hillsides of my native land.

My other duties included cleaning the chopping blocks on Saturday night; "boning out" necks, shanks, and similar animal parts for hamburger; occasionally reaching shoulder deep into the biting sub-zero cold of the brine barrel, hoping so hopefully to come up at the first dive with the morsel desired, were it beef tongue, pig's foot or whatever.

Incidentally, directly back of the meat market, facing Main Street, was the "telephone office" where most telephone calls were initiated at this time. Mae Starrett McLain, the butcher's sister, was the efficient chief of the switchboards. And another sister, the gentle Alta (Luttrell), was the ticket sales girl at the movie house.

To the right (west) of the butcher shop was Dad McFadden's Hotel and Restaurant. I believe it was then or earlier called Central Hotel. Earlier it had been operated by W. H. Graham whom I do not remember.

The sign over the hotel porch roof says: Meals at all Hours.

Another sign on the window below read: Steaks and Chops. I know because I painted it there. That kind of work could have kept me busy, but it was a little too exacting for me. Inside the restaurant a sign on the wall proclaimed: Regular meals 35 cents; Square meals 50 cents; Royal Gorge one dollar.

I believe it is generally recognized that country bred boys and girls, especially those with farm experience, become acquainted earlier than city children with the inexorable facts of life, death, and general calamity. Yet I cannot say that I have ever enjoyed the necessity of butchering chickens or animals, or even killing wild ones.

I was too young to be heavily impressed by seeing Santa Claus seriously burned (as later described). But the tragedy of December 26, 1915, still saddens me. It was a quiet Sunday morning and a small crowd was awaiting the noon train and the arrival of city papers. I was standing in front of the butcher shop watching seven year old Harry Olney, only child of Judge and Mrs. Olney, playing tag with other kids.

Down the street very slowly in his new Studebaker auto drove "Old Bill" Carr, vice president of the bank. Suddenly the auto and young Harry collided. Roy Yarbrough and Charlie Thorpe picked up the unconscious child and rushed him to the doctor's house. He had been killed almost instantly.

No one ever questioned the driver's inability to avoid the accident. But I noted several times thereafter that when Mr. Carr crossed that place in the street he never did so without pausing a moment to look down. Once I heard a moan of anguish escape from his lips.

Before departing from the brick building area reference should be made to the cement sidewalk. For nearly twenty years this was the only such sidewalk in town. And it ended at the edge of the later theater building. Where there were other sidewalks they were constructed of 2 by 6 inch wooden planks. Often such adjoining sidewalks were set at different levels. The planks were rarely tight together after a few years weathering. A sidewalk crack makes an ideal coin trap. And small boys made it their business to scout the trap lines for lost coins to be retrieved by chewing gum on the end of a stick.

Another boys' ritual was the regular scrutiny of water troughs for the chance spontaneous generation of horsehair snakes. It was just as well that no naturalist tried to convince us that the jet black round worms were actually cousins of the nematods named *Paragordius varius*. After all, everyone in town knew where horses were brought to drink. And when a course black hair from a horse's mane starts to wiggle — how smart do you have to be?

6
Entertainment

THE social, political and religious behavior and attitudes of the Guerneville settlers of the first several decades must have reflected their place of origin. That would have embraced practically the entire nation, but mostly the midwest. These pioneers worked hard and probably the majority drank hard.

The more "cultural" community gatherings included church socials, picnics, band concerts and locally produced stage skits and lime-lighted *tableaux vivants*. Out of doors, especially on such holidays as the Fourth of July, there were turkey shoots and bull team races. Oxen were always referred to as bulls in the redwoods. There was a town baseball team which ebbed and flowed in activity. I have an early memory of sitting in the grass near out-fielder Roy Smith during a game. The field then was on the west side of Mayes Canyon Road and north of Pocket Creek. Redwood stumps must have been a nuisance.

A town of this nature would often produce some unusually fine natural athletes. With discipline and training they could no doubt have become professionals. But most of them would tolerate neither. I am inclined to believe that their attitude reflected the bold individuality of the frontier. However, with that attitude went increased personal responsibility for individual behavior.

During the administration of Roosevelt the Rough Rider, Guerneville on the Russian River was an isolated little village, especially during winter. This was in spite of the two passenger trains passing through daily. Passenger arrivals and departures constituted the social highlight of each day. And the arrival of a new bride and groom was echoed through the woody canyons by the locomotive whistle miles ahead of the oncoming train.

Those countrymen who could not make it to the railroad station were thus forewarned of the inevitable noisy charivari (shivaree) to be held that same evening around, over, and eventually within the residence of the newlyweds, often quite contrary to the wishes of the bridegroom and undoubtedly to the embarrassment of the bride.

Local stage entertainment was furnished by local talent, and especially by school children. A truly valuable cultural experience for such small towns was the occasional appearance of the Chatauqua shows. Rarely, a small animal circus would venture that far into the hinterlands. Small troupes of repertory players would often appear for several night stands. Their plays were most often the old melodramas of the period; and the dubious talent of the actors no doubt accounted for their assignment of such low degree. It would be only fair to point out, however, that during this golden era of vaudeville there must have been literally thousands of actors of no particular talent continuously criss-crossing the nation, appearing in the several theater circuits.

Kerosene lamps furnished illumination and, quite naturally for this community, wood fuel was used for cooking and heating. A few of the most affluent families possessed wind-up graphaphones or a magic lantern. The latter device was no different from the modern slide projector except that the lack of a strong and concentrated source of light sometimes caused a problem. The more efficient of these projectors used carbide gas to produce a brilliant flame behind the glass slide. Carbide was used to light the headlights of the earliest automobiles. This gas was created by the mixing of a solid chemical and water. The elements could therefore be transported in small quantity, and gas produced as needed.

Movies had first been shown to the public in New York City in the year 1894. Naturally, the first projections were flickering novelties rather than dramatic works of art. It was not until 1911 that any type of story longer than a single reel (about 15 minutes showing time) was manufactured in the new medium.

My first encounter with moving pictures is vividly remembered. It probably occurred in 1907 or 1908 at the famous old Chutes at the Beach of San Francisco. In some dark and narrow sideshow a steaming, smoking locomotive careened out of the distance, straight at the audience which included this small, terrified and howling country boy. Older brother George saved the boy's life by promptly escorting him to daylight. This was no epic story of the iron horse portrayed on the silver screen. Unquestionably, the simple fact of moving pictures on a white wall attracted a side-show crowd of that era.

I believe there were some commercial showings of hand-tinted glass slides in our village piror to the introduction of motion pictures. I do not remember them, however. Probably house painter Daniel Boone Brians became the first movie mogul of Guerneville, but for a brief period only. Considerable research in old newspapers fails to reveal the date of this business venture. The year must have been about 1909.

Such electricity as might have been generated locally was not powerful enough, and no light globe was yet perfected, which would adequately project the film image onto a screen a modest distance away. Therefore, limelight was used. This combination of oxyhydrogen flame and lime made a brilliant light which had long been utilized for footlights and theater spotlights. The film was chemically akin to gunpowder and highly inflammable. The short reels of film were ground through the projection machine by hand, and generally collected in a wicker clothes basket below.

I have no idea if Brians' "nickelodeon" had any particular name, nor how long it was in existence. It was situated between the Guerneville Hotel and Martha Hansen's Bakery, facing west on Cinnabar Avenue, that is, across from the Louvre. I have two clear, brief and fixed memory pictures of the theater.

I was standing with big brother Clarence by the water trough as he tried to explain what was going on in the lighted building across the street. Of course, I had no comprehension of this new miracle of the entertainment world. I was a very small boy, at most five years old. We seemed to have wandered down Railroad Avenue and returned when my second clear memory impression was fixed. The theater had become a vivid yellow-orange box of flame. Strangely, the concept of fire, heat or danger did not seem to register upon me. My third memory impression of the event was set on the stage of the Louvre Saloon porch. Dan Brians was there, his arms swathed in white bandages. He was naturally the center of attraction as he explained what had happened.

What had happened was the complete loss of the theater and adjoining Martha Hanson's Bakery. The south face of the Hotel suffered a deep charring. These scars probably still could be found below the recent application of stucco.

The second moving picture theater is well remembered, but I

cannot place it precisely in time or place. The year was around 1910 to 1912 and about where the old locomotive turntable had been, that is, north of the track between Church and Mill streets. It had a very brief existence.

The barn theater had no floor except hard earth and the seats were straight wooden benches without backs. The small boy sat on the bench waiting. There were other townspeople sitting about, also waiting. But the only action seemed to be coming from Gene Pells who was the official helper of the theater manager. Gene was the grandson of James Pells, one of the earliest pioneers into this area. At this time his family lived at the south end of Lone Mountain on the west bank of Fife Creek by the old Guerne hop kiln. Later Gene was one of the half dozen Guerneville youths, including my brothers, who promptly marched off to the First World War by enlisting aboard the ill-fated Cruiser San Diego. (The vessel went down off New England, undoubtedly the result of internal bomb sabotage.)

On that night when the little steam engine outside the barn theater refused to operate and generate electricity for the moving pictures, Gene came forth and stood before the small audience. Recognizing his importance at this moment of history, Gene told all by declaring seriously, "Folks, she's on the blink."

The third commercial enterprise was much more successful. In the year 1911 a new resident to the community built another barn-like structure strictly in the shape best suited for audience viewing of moving pictures. The man was William S. Smith, more commonly called English Smith because he and his family were straight out of Kipling. The Smiths lived on the Drake Road (which was very thinly settled then) just eastward from Bert Guerne's Southside Resort.

The Smith Theatorium was constructed at the Guerneville end of the bridge on the east (upriver) side. On the other side of the bridge stood the Oak Run Saloon of Fred Ringwald. Immediately north, that is, between the theater and the railroad track and fronting on Cinnabar Avenue stood one of the most important establishments of the community. This was Noel Tunstall's Livery Stable. At about this stage of world history the needs of the automobile were being considered as well as the care and "hiring" of horses. On the right side of the large entry door was a well equipped harness shop and office, smelling of leather and neatsfoot oil. On the left side, George Weber and Clifford Marshall were learning the hot process of vulcanizing inner tubes.

Under the theater, which was at the lower end some ten feet above ground, a few swine minded their particular business, without creating any objection from the patrons.

The theater floor sloped down at an angle of perhaps five degrees. Folding chairs were bolted to the floor; but not all of the chairs. Screws holding down the first several rows had been industriously removed by small boys. The apparent advantage, other than simple mischief, was found in the opportunity for the urchins to lie back on the tilted seats and look almost straight up at the flickering screen and the open rafters festooned with cobwebs. The adult audience kept itself well back in the theater, probably in order to separate itself from the continuous yowling and running commentary arising from the front seats. This became sheer riot whenever animals, and especially wild animals appeared on the screen. The adults were dubiously aided in their acoustical relief by the flat tinkle and jangle of an electric piano at the rear of the theater which pursued its unbroken course entirely unrelated to the pathos or comedy of life being emoted on the silent screen.

Being now at the rear, or proper entrance to the theater (no emergency exits are remembered to have existed) it would appear more logical to set the stage in this direction before regretfully returning to an unpleasant incident involving the pride and future hope of Guerneville—now raising cain down in the front seats.

Consider first the balcony. This was a dark box, a left over space adjoining the projection room and above the tintinabulating piano. The only access was by way of a vertical ladder against the wall. Possibly twenty seats were available. This was not the glittering dress circle. Whatever may have been the original intent of English Smith, this isolation ward served very well to accommodate the unwashed. Peanut shells were never less than ankle deep on the floor. A dank perfume of garlic and alcoholic spirits was fortunately light enough to rise into the rafters above.

The peanut shells were a by-product of another substantial institution of free enterprise. Near the theater door and within his wheeled, glass-sided "peanut wagon" was seated Pop Damon. Pop sold bags of the fresh roasted product to the theater-goers. I was also aware that he carried a potato in his pocket to ward off rheumatism.

By this date the long feature movie of five reels was common, although shorter pictures were also run. Mary Pickford's publicity agents had succeeded in having her recognized as America's Sweetheart; and there was the indestructable Pauline, left miraculously dangling in some Peril at the close of each performance. But the stalwarts (or so the small boy would have testified) were the comedians John Bunny, Flora Finch, Sidney Drew and his wife, and Ham and Bud. Elmo Lincoln performed prodigious feats of strength. Charlie Chaplin and Bill Hart were on the near horizon. The silent crowing rooster of Pathé News was already a familiar introduction to the living picture record of worldwide events.

The showing of still slides was a common practice in movie theaters of that time. This occurred during such emergencies as broken films, and regularly as a local advertising venture. Two such hand-tinted glass slides remain clear in this writer's memory. One showed the patrician profile of an elegant Gibson Girl bedecked with wide brimmed ostrich plume hat. With it came the printed message: "Ladies will remove their hats." Another slide declared: "Gentlemen will not, and others must not smoke during the performance."

The youth of today is not likely to recognize the impact of silent motion pictures during that period of the Nation's history. The isolated village might have heretofore been privileged to view one or two mediocre traveling stage shows during the year.

Now, by the second decade of the Century the outside world of fact and the shining dream world of the theater were available several times a week, right there for not more than a quarter dollar admission fee.

By this time the electric carbon arc was available to throw a shaft of light several hundred feet with great efficiency. The principal projection specialist of the Smith theater was William, the second of the three small town mechanical genuises, the Marshall brothers. Bill was also the general manager; and Bill suffered from the indignities perpetrated by the boys down in front. From adequate personal experience as a onetime urchin in the same environment, Bill realized that a direct attack would lead only to his own defeat.

Down near the front row of seats at the floor level was a hole in the wall, possibly cut out to improve the ventilation. Bill knew perfectly well that some of his smallest but most enthusiastic customers were entering upon the premises without purchasing a ticket from Gladys Bagley, cashier at the front door. They simply shinnied up a foundation pier and crawled through the hole.

The principal actor in the small life drama here related shall remain unnamed simply because in maturity he so vehemently denies the part he played. Consider the costume of the small boy of that place and time. In summer it generally consisted of nothing other than faded, bibbed blue overalls, with sometimes a shirt. That was sufficient. But our hero of the moment also proudly displayed an elaborate bartender's vest, buttoned around the bib of his overalls. It was (or had been) an elegant white material peppered with tiny green shamrocks — a thing of beauty until that particular night. For William Marshall had, with malice afore-thought, under cover of early twilight, smeared the common route of entry with a rich mixture of pig filth. Our young hero, demon-strating his usual aggressive spirit had been the first to make a flying leap at the foundation timber, only to slide ingloriously to the ground below.

At about this time, that is around 1914, another movie house or nickelodeon was built on First (or more properly Main) Street near the later entrance to Johnson's Camp Grounds. This was operated by partners Byrd McPeak and one Nordman. The McPeaks were an early family in the river area, whose name lingers at the isolated little cemetery at Hacienda. This theater remained only a couple of years and left no distinguishing imprint upon world history.

Hollywood had become the glittering world capital of a fan-tastic new communication medium. With a river of box-office money such early geniuses as Griffith and DeMille were learning to spread their wings. First the big city cinema palaces and then the most remote watertank towns were able to display such super-colossal spectaculars as *Broken Blossoms, The Eyes of the World,*

Daughter of the Gods, and *The Naked Truth.* This open door to cultural revolution could not long avoid public controversy arising with the creation of such pictures as *Where Are My Children?* and *The Clansmen.*

And still the dreamers dreamed; even of such impossible things as talking moving pictures and of pictures presented in natural colors.

About 1916 Leland S. Murphy bought out the interest of English Smith, and proceeded to construct an excellent movie theater for a town of that size. Lee was born on the hill. He was the son of Frank and Docia Murphy. The theater was equipped with a stage and Wurlitzer Organ. Murphy even hired a young but well qualified artist to paint an interior decorative frieze. Robert Howard (son of the eminent architect John Galen Howard) recorded his characterizations of many townspeople in his high frieze down the side walls. How unfortunate that this small bit of memorabilia has been destroyed and lost.

This new theater was built at the site of the first railway station, that is, immediately adjoining the Odd Fellows brick building as seen in Photo C. Clifford (Casey) Marshall assumed the responsibility of first operating the projection machines. By this date, very powerful incandescent globes had come to replace the sputtering, white-hot carbon arc lights behind the film. In the summer of 1917 Casey joined the Coast Artillery. This writer and Joe Buttner then assumed the work of operating the machines and handling film shipments.

At this time, 1916-18, this area itself was lightly touched by the magic of Hollywood. The Middleton brothers were somehow cousins of the Guernes and they had been active in lumbering here and there near Guerneville. About 1916 one of them launched himself into movie production, renamed his actress wife Beatriz Michelini and took his small company to Korbel Vineyard to shoot some scenes from the immortal *Faust.*

I doubt if the final release exceeded Grade B. But I do remember the beauty of the scenery they had chosen. The autumn leaves of the grapes there were blood red among the black redwood stumps. They had imported the last working ox team from somewhere along the coast to haul the grape harvest up to the cameras.

As a self-invited observer, and with my developing interest in the graphic arts, I was much impressed.

Then about a year later a much bigger visitation from Hollywood descended upon Vacation Beach, downriver about three miles from town. The novel *The Money Master* by Sir Gilbert Parker was being produced under the movie title *The Wise Fool*. James Kirkwood was the star. He was an authentic matinee idol of the era, and he acted the haughty role off-stage as well as before the camera. Many of the townspeople, were hired as extras to populate the French Canadian villa fabricated on Vacation Beach. The grand finale was the evening burning of the villa. Many of us watched this performance from across the river. The final production was a better than average movie of the time.

Photo F could have been made on May Day, 1908. The occasion obviously called for a public celebration, and the boys were of that age class. The photographer was looking generally southwest. Behind him was the Congregational Church. This was the west end of Old Main Street.

To the right about 200 feet the street ended at the elaborate gates of what we called Westover Park. The big mill had been abandoned for a half-dozen years now and only the huge sawdust pile remained. Someone had carelessly allowed a trash fire to sneak into the sawdust five or six years after this picture was made. That caused a summer smoke nuisance for nearly a decade as well as a most hazardous surface area. Such fires have been known to smolder for 20 years or longer. Fortunately, and unexpectedly, a high flood extinguished the sawdust fire. That was probably the great flood of 1920-21.

The old photo is stained and cracked. But it is obvious that the boys are standing among low street weeds. This indicates the lack of both travel and nibbling by waiting mules or horses.

I feel sure that the neat white house beyond the mules housed the office of the town's dentist. I cannot remember his name, but I do remember him separating me from what must have been baby teeth.

To the right of the photographer was the home and office of

Photo F: The Pool boys and Buster Clar on lower Main Street, circa 1908.

Doctor Schmelz and also an Attorney named McGuffin. The attorney had a daughter named Allie. I remember little of her as a person, undoubtedly because she was female and I was the four or five year old boy bringing up the rear in the photo.

I am not sure if she owned the little cart with the parasol, but the Teddy Bear passenger belonged to her. He came equipped with a pocket handkerchief. Along the parade route several viewers advised me to blow Teddy's nose. Apparently nothing so fixes the abiding memory patterns as do those events which provoke personal embarrassment. I believe such an influence will prevail even when one is simply a witness of embarrassment or sorrow inflicted upon another person.

My float won a prize. Perhaps they all did. At any rate, a few days later I was sent to answer a knock on our front door. There stood Mrs. Cobb. I said, "My mother isn't home."

She said, "I have come to see you. And here is the 25 cents prize you won with your parade float."

This busy woman had walked at least a half mile, including up the hill and steep steps a couple of city blocks in length, to deliver the silver coin prize (one hour labor wage of the time) to a preschool urchin. Therein must exist a lesson in citizenship worthy of contemplation in any era.

In respect to the boys' hats, this was the era of "Buster Brown and his dog Tige" in newspaper comics. Undoubtedly, that is where I acquired the nickname, Buster. By that name alone was I recognized in my home town; and still am by a few elders. Yet I am positive that *my* "Buster Brown flat hat" was genuine Navy issue, a present from a second cousin after his service in the recent Spanish American War. Wherever the hat went, I was under it.

The boy sitting in the wagon is Clarence Lea Pool, always called Bullfrog because of his webbed toes. Left front is elder brother Elmer Jacob Pool. Perhaps the other boy was yet an older brother Elbert (Buzz). Their grandparents Pool were pioneer settlers on Pool Ridge west of town and to the north of Gabe's Rock.

"Jake" eventually retired after a career in the State Park Service. He was a bright, alert youngster, pretty much into everything. I cannot resist telling of one event where his forwward nature clearly reacted to his personal embarrassment. At any rate he came up with a very red face.

The hilarious small town incident occurred some ten years after the parade picture was taken. Jake volunteered joyfully to substitute as a driver in a wagon parade of an itinerant Uncle Tom's Cabin Show. He was dressed in a man's outsize gray uniform with red stripes. Down Main Street lumbered the several circus wagons drawn by large draft horses. On each wagon top several dogs bellowed like the hounds of hell. And there was the Pride of Guerneville, with little of his face showing from his retreat into the gray coat collar and oversized cap. At each of Jake's ears a great slobbering monster earned his hamburger by barking as though the Russians were again ascending the river. The volunteer driver had not been told that the huge dogs got warmed up here for chasing poor Liza across the ice at the evening performance. I don't remember if I cried at Liza's cruel fate. But I do remember how I laughed at Elmer Jacob that day.

It is possible that a parenthetical observation at this point in respect to such typical small town humor may be of some scholarly value. First, it is freely admitted that no written description, regardless of its eloquence, could possibly substitute for viewing the original performance. The point the writer wishes to make is that the innocent, unplanned aspect of the incident sets it aside from the bulk of professional laugh-making humor which is (or was, before television) the more common fare of the city dweller. Secondly, it is submitted that the essence of such folksy humor is almost entirely dependent upon the mutual familiarity of the respective innocent actors and their audience. This can exist best only in a small and cohesive community.

The Guerneville Band in Armstrong Grove in 1886. After a lapse of activity another town band was formed about 1915. Fred Warne was leader. The departure of young men to war in 1917 started its decline.

The picture of Guerneville Band was taken in Armstrong Grove in 1886. Sixth from the left is Herbert Lincoln Bagley, son of John W. the pioneer. Bert was a dignified banker, devoted family man and good judge of whiskey. I am surprised that he held a cornet here rather than his beloved baritone horn. Bert used to tell of the time he stood on the roof of Odd Fellows Hall to "echo" certain melodies arising from the band on the street below. When it came time to sound the mellow echoes his horn was mute. Some joker had stuffed the instrument with wads of paper.

I remember walking past the bank one day with my mother. Perhaps I was nine years of age. The dignified banker stepped out, bowed and said, "How do you do Mrs. Clar."

"How do you do, Mr. Bagley, and how are you feeling?"

"To tell the truth, I am not very well. You know, Mrs. Clar, when I was a boy I went to sea. While I was stranded on the docks at St. Petersburg my toes froze. I cut them off and threw them into the Baltic Sea. I believe that now I am beginning to suffer from that event."

To the (photo) right of Bert is my father Ivon Clar, band leader at this time. Second and third to the right of Ivon are the lean Arthur Turner and dumpy Omer Cobb.

I remember the bright red uniforms striped with gold down the trouser legs and at the shoulders. Probably all the remaining uniforms were burned in the brick building during the fire of 1963. Incidentally, this lively band traveled to San Francisco in 1898 to assist in welcoming home the soldiers from the Phillipines.

I faintly remember the band in uniform in Armstrong Grove. It is interesting that these earliest memories are all in the shape of clear and colorful pictures, without sound and generally so brief as to portray no sense of continued motion. I remember principally my father approaching us, smiling and with cornet in hand. Probably on that same day occurred the incident of my being pulled up by my arms between the front and rear wheels of a light surrey "with a fringe on top." I was set down beside my mother and another woman. They were attired in flouncy long dresses, wide hats and parasols which indicated some gala occasion. Yet I actually believe my fear of the front wheel turning in to crush me, as it really could have, caused that particular picture to be

89

stamped in my memory. I would guess that I was three years of age.

Possibly another memory picture was recorded that same day. There was a Maypole Dance in Armstrong Grove. Six or eight brightly clad small girls were spinning colorful ribbons around a decorated pole. The brief frozen memory picture somehow lets me believe that half the children were dancing in one direction and the others oppositely as each wrapped her long ribbon around the Maypole. One wonders if those who enjoyed the innocent spring-time dance on that day so long ago were actually aware that they were celebrating the tree worshipers rituals of fertility and prosperity which can be traced throughout all of Europe back into dim antiquity.

Mention was made elsewhere about the Temperance Society meetings in early Guerneville. Probably as early as 1880, that group and others used Armstrong Grove for conferences and picnics. For example, I attended an elaborate picnic sponsored by the entire community for a detail of about 30 sailors from Mare Island during the First World War.

In the early years the common use of the grove was an entirely unregulated courtesy on the part of Colonel James B. Armstrong, and then his heirs. I have no recollection of that gentleman or his wife, but daughter Lizzie Armstrong Jones was a familiar character. Actually, her wind-broken bay mare was the most recognizable character as she trotted along the Mines Road, grunting loudly at every step.

Armstrong wished to donate the original 640 acre property to some public agency for perpetual use as a botanical park. This was in 1892 and neither legal machinery nor public interest existed. In 1909 the State Legislature was prevailed upon to pass an appro-priation of $100,000 to purchase the remaining 400 acres. Governor Gillett vetoed the bill. In 1913 local people started a county-wide campaign, and by 1917 persuaded the Supervisors to purchase the grove for $70,000. The heirs contributed land worth $10,000. Bob Coon was the first county caretaker, and then Ed Pells. In 1934 the park was transferred to State jurisdiction.

7

Team Bells in the Night, and Magnesite

THERE was another large, shed-like structure below and beyond the Theatorium and the livery stable. That would be on the river bench east of the end of the bridge, and below the present post office. For many years a lumber yard has been in operation there. The original shed structure was not built there for that purpose. Its origin had to do with magnesite.

Presumably the great war in Europe stimulated magnesite mining as it did the production of quicksilver. On East Austin Creek the Sonoma Magnesite Company located eight or ten adjoining claims running from one to three miles above Red Slide. This was very isolated country, six miles to Cazadero and 12 miles to Guerneville toward the southeast. By mid-1915 this company employed 70 men and operated a calcining plant near the quarry. By that date its eight mile, 24 inch gauge railroad was hauling the product to Watson Station where it was reloaded onto regular narrow gauge cars. Thence it was hauled to Duncans for further loading onto N.W.P.R.R. freight cars. In 1916 excessive cost caused the operation to cease.

This operation touched Guerneville in two respects, both related to transportation. It must have been in 1914 that six town youths were hired to work on the survey of the lilliputian railroad up Austin Creek past Rocky Mountain. Three of them contracted typhoid fever and were dreadfully ill. One was Older Brother George; another was Jack Coon, who was to die of influenza during his service in the Navy; the third was the English-born Duncan Smith. In fact, this illness was directly accountable for Duncan's unusual war adventures. A doctor recommended a sea voyage to regain his health. Quite unknowingly he signed on as radio operator on a Mexican flag vessel which was actually a secret collier for German submarine raiders in Pacific waters. He foiled some German plans — but that was only the beginning of his story which was published serially in the S.F. *Examiner*.

Incidentally, one of the young men who did not suffer any ill effect from drinking Austin Creek water was the same Ben Roberts who is honored elsewhere in this writing.

Before the little railroad was built and before the heavy magnesite ore was processed near the quarry, the ore had been sacked and hauled to Guerneville. There it was loaded onto freight cars for rail shipment. Hauling the ore wagons by four or six horse teams over the Morrison, the Dutton, and the Gilliam grades must have been brutal work. I don't know how much time the twelve mile haul required. What I do remember was being awakened during the silent nights by the jangling bells of the lead horses of each team. Their passage along the Mines Road was just below our house. They were then no more than a half mile from the freight depot and rest.

The bells were used on long teams in the days of heavy burdens over narrow mountain roads as a warning to approaching travelers. Light wagons must select a place to pass. Both lead horses usually carried on their collars the upstanding frame with either six or twelve little brass bells. The high brassy clanging of these bells could not be mistaken. As the plodding animal weaved from side to side the team bells cried, "Ka-janng, ka-janng" into the mountain stillness.

Of course, there were no lights permitted on the wagons to interfere with the horse's adequate night vision. Sidelamps for wagons became a legal requirement a few years later because of the increasing number of automobiles on the roads. Therefore, a special little kerosene lamp, with a red glass at the rear, was fastened on the left side of horse drawn vehicles. Quite naturally, old-timers considered them more nuisance than help.

That long, long age of the noble, stupid servant of man has departed irrevocably, and in what seems in retrospect to have happened during a very short time period. The great urbanization of the nation has caused the horse to be known essentially only on the bridal path and at the race track or rodeo. I have no particular personal regrets. But I was impressed recently with the point I have just made when I asked my 15 year old grandson how he thought a teamster of old would unload a wagon carrying a ton of sand, dirt or gravel. He seemed genuinely interested in the explanation. Then it occurred to me that never again in this country will a 15 year old boy labor as I have labored at unloading such a wagon. The floor of the wagon bed was composed of boards of about 2 by 4 inch dimension set lengthwise, with the ends shaved a little to make a handle. First, one outside plank was turned on its edge to let some of the gravel slide through to the ground. Then the next and the next, until all of the floor planks were on edge. At the end, the entire load would lie in a pile under the wagon frame. From such small and perishable memories is woven the history of a great nation's past.

We had been discussing the shed-like structure east of the bridge and below the present post office, and how the business of magnesite mining was involved. The building and what was called a stack kiln were built in 1917. This was the plant of Western Carbonic Acid Gas Company, owned and managed by the Harker family. I remember talking to the self-satisfied old gentleman when his family lived at the Guerneville Hotel that year.

The company controlled magnesite claims at the head of Gilliam Creek. That would be directly north of town some six or seven miles, and over the Jackson Ridge. By this time, motorized trucks had supplanted horses, and I once rode such a truck to and from these claims. Brother George was working on road construction near the quarry. Harker senior died before the operation was well under way and all work ceased. However, there was some very light magnesia produced from the very heavy magnesite ore.

The next venture to occupy the big building was so unusual as to be almost unbelievable. It was commonly referred to as the "stump factory." I cannot remember the company name. The date of operation was about 1921. I remember a community meeting in the schoolhouse one evening. Company chemists and promoters were explaining the process and endeavoring to sell stock. And they did sell some.

The object was to treat redwood stump material so as to extract carbolic and phenol and other chemicals beyond my knowledge. Old redwood heartwood harbored the chemicals and Old Stumptown could furnish the stumps. I believe the promoters were technically correct and sincere. The project was a business failure for the same reason the magnesite mines had ceased operation. Combined production and distribution costs exceeded profits.

Stump pulled out of Guerne's field by two horses and block and tackle.

Many large and solid stumps were removed from the Big Bottom and on other land being converted to agricultural use. This land clearing labor is well recorded in the picture of the big stump on its side. It was taken on the Guerne Ranch in the vicinity of the old Livreau sawmill, about year 1916. The man at the top is Sam Mazzola and the other is Charlie Bean, both faithful longtime employees of George Guerne.

Removing such large stumps required much hard and often dangerous work. Redwoods do not produce a single strong tap root, as is obvious in this picture. That fact has given rise to a ridiculous legend regarding the almost total lack of roots in this species. The truth is that redwoods produce a greater volume of wood structure below ground than above. The numerous roots are widespread. That condition requires the knowledgeable redwood stump remover to strive to avoid shattering stump and upper roots in the removal process. Otherwise he has the job of chopping out root segments remaining above plow depth.

Most stumps were removed with blasting powder or dynamite. And the rule was to never stint on the inital charges of explosives. Two hundred sticks of dynamite might be used on a stump of this size. An accomplished "powder man" is a skilled technician.

The stump in the picture was pulled over by two sturdy horses winding a steel cable around a winch or capstan spool. That operation was little less dangerous than the use of explosives. Older Brother George missed death by inches when the very rig shown in the picture snapped a line and threw a steel pulley block just over his head as he hugged Mother Earth.

Small boys and newcomers around taut cable work have long heard a warning that eventually became a part of the vernacular language. A common bit of advice was, "Stay out of the bight of the line."

I learned the hard way the literal value of that warning. Twice I was hit by cables suddenly snapped under pressure.

One day when I was about thirteen, I was visiting a "one-man stump puller" job where my brothers were laboring at converting natural forest land into a fruit orchard. In the end their weary labor proved to be futile. The point of the moment concerns the snapping of the half-inch cable under the pressure of the capstan's bar they were pushing. The end tip of the wild steel line struck me at the base of my skull. The accident frightened the three Clar brothers exceedingly but did no serious damage.

A second experience came near being fatal. A large redwood butt log was being pulled down a gulch toward a steam donkey. Dirt plowed up in front of the log brought it to a stubborn halt. I was working too near the inch and a half mainline when a swivel "dog" hook in the log snapped from the pressure. The cable whipped out, skinned my back, and threw me behind a log I was sawing up for donkey fuel. The log prevented my being cut in half by that awful stinger. The incident took place during my summer vacation of 1925. I was working at probably the last small logging operation near Guerneville in a remnant of the virgin redwood. It was near Hollydale Park as I remember.

In my later life I admit to having always felt a bit uncomfortable whenever I have found myself standing in the near presence of a steel cable under tension.

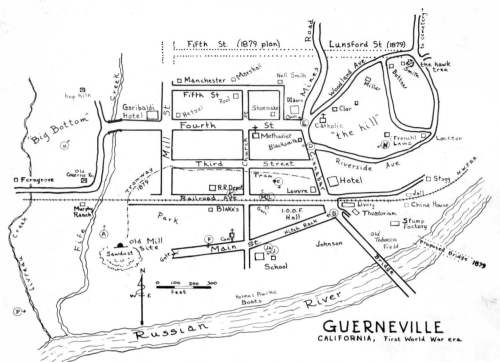

Sketch map of Guerneville at the time of First World War.

The plat of Guerneville shown here is essentially the product of this writer's memory as well as his hand. It was intended to represent the village of his youth, including some of the principal streets and structures mentioned in this discussion.

The camera location of most of the reproduced photographs are shown by a circled letter. Street names are strictly those used prior to the time that changes in some names were officially made by the Board of Supervisors, about 1960.

There is one important addition in this plat, showing features which did not in fact exist. They are indicated by dotted lines. These features were taken from a "Plan of the Town of Guerneville," filed with the County Recorder on November 20, 1879. The survey work was done in 1875-76 by civil engineers Davis and Cox. On that plat the present Fifth Street was labeled an alley. Note the proposed Fifth Street and Lunsford Street 150 feet north of present Fifth Street. Note the tramway to the sawmill which existed when the 1879 map was made. Note also the proposed bridge across the river about a hundred yards north of

96

the current selected crossing of 1882. Presumably the summer bridge, over which so much lumber was transported, was located at the upriver site in 1875.

At the early date, the later Cinnabar (Armstrong Woods Road) was labeled only a "public road." Present Main Street (Old Railroad Avenue) was originally termed Second Street. The reason for the narrow width of present Church Street is found on the Plan of 1879. It was intended that this be a mere alley extending from the river north to Third Street. Significantly, however, directly north of this alley to proposed Fifth Street were 25 foot lots. Clearly, the surveyors provided for the extension of Church Street "alley" as far north as the town cared to expand. The proposed cemetery was indicated up on the hill around the present Laws home. And the only road proposed to reach that site was the indicated Lunsford Street, which would have required a very steep climb straight east from the Mines Road to the big French Tree on the hill.

Photo Nd: From the hill about 1900. This was essentially the town of the author's earliest recollections. The mill was gone after 1901. But there is Tunstall's Livery Stable at far left and the rear of the Guerneville Hotel at near center. To its right is an embryo Third Street and the van der Straten house. At far right is the Methodist Church. Beyond "the brick building" are the schoolhouse and Congregational Church. The center of town is an open lot. All the hills have been logged.

Photo D: John Coon at his hardware store about 1913.

Photo E: The Coon residence about 1913.

8

Cinnabar Avenue

PHOTOS D and E feature the John T. Coon business and residence around 1913. In both cases the camera was aimed generally northwest from the middle of Cinnabar Avenue (now Armstrong Woods Road). Of course, if you had asked Mr. Coon (in Photo D) or Mrs. Coon or her sister Rose (in Photo E) they probably would have hesitated to tell you the street names. I suspect that some residents were not aware that any street other than Main had been honored with a particular name. The reason was simple. Who needs street names when every house resident is well known? And, of course, there were no street signs.

John Coon was an industrious business man, a devoted father and community leader. He was rarely seen without the black derby hat covering his bald head. My family and his were very close, so that I remember him well and with great respect.

The hardware store and the blacksmith shop (behind the car) were once joined. I believe an early Coon residence stood where the store is in the picture, until moved across the street where it still exists. During the years 1884 through 1890, Robert Wilson Coon, with his son John as sometime partner, fabricated plows, wagons and farm implements at this location.

During all of my childhood, from about age three to 15 years, I trudged past the blacksmith shop between home and "downtown," often several times a day. Most of the things I remember about that minute part of the world are naturally very personal and generally so inconsequential as to cause wonder why they have rated a file card for six decades in the incomprehensible memory system of one brain.

The space between store and smithy collected many fascinating odds and ends of tools and devices common to rural America of the early Twentieth Century. The dominant feature, however, was the elevator platform used to "freeze" red hot iron wagon tires onto wooden wheel rims. The platform could be raised and lowered in a pit about a foot deep. A hot tire would be carried rapidly away from the inside forge by several men. Then it would be lowered carefully over the wheel. The supporting platform was dropped into water in the pit. This would shrink the rim, and possibly have some tempering effect at the same time.

This performance was a great show for small boys. In fact, the town blacksmith shop was a primary action center. Runner-up competition for the attention of idlers and youth was the railroad station at train time and the livery stable.

Billy Miller, the smithy and farrier, was a congenial soul, tolerant of small boys, idlers, and the occasional borrowers of tools and horseshoe nails. Billy was not a large man, but he was unquestionably as tough as rawhide and twice as strong. He was somewhat palsied, with cramped fingers and knees, probably muscle-bound after long years of lifting great weights, swinging hammers, and clamping horses fetlocks firmly between his knees as he shod them.

Competent small town blacksmiths had to be talented craftsman. I wonder if Billy would seem so to the unknowing youth of our jet airplane age? His clothes and old felt hat were black from smoke and cinders; his heavy leather apron was streaked with burn scars from the forge. His eyes were red from drifting smoke.

There was no heat vent over the forge. I have been told that blacksmiths objected to drafts around their anvil which might interfere with the precise temperature they could see in the orange metal in their tongs. The brick chimney seen in the old picture served a heating stove in the small corner office. Smoke arising from the forge eventually drifted through the roof shingles.

Note the low plank flooring at street level. Smithy floors were continuously abused by movement of heavy objects and heavy horses. Furthermore, a raised wooden floor presented a hazard where fire and sparks were so common. Over the floor were strewn tools, remnants of mill iron, and coal clinkers, and pared chunks of horse's hooves, and nails and bolts.

Some orderliness around the anvil and water barrel was to be seen in the racks of special tongs and hammers, the barrels of new horseshoes and a sack of hard "blacksmith coal." But no winter draft through the always open door could dampen the mingled odor of horse manure, and urine, pungent coal smoke and acrid odor of singed hoof under the final fitting of a hot horseshoe.

Throughout the long work day a passerby could hear the

throaty moaning of the hand-powered forge bellows or a sizzling iron thrust into the slack barrel; and over all the happily singing anvil as Billy Miller tap-tapped a light rhythm before each sharp stroke that spewed sparks from white iron.

Small wonder that every anxious mother thought first of the village smithy in the absence of her wandering man-child.

The automobile in the photograph was declared by two experts of the Horseless Carriage Club to have been a Cadillac Roadster built about year 1910.* The dominating position of this vehicle in the picture is prophetic. Around 1927 the blacksmith shop was closed permanently. And the hardware store was converted into a garage to repair the increasing number of gasoline powered vehicles.

Joe Santos was not a native Indian as many people believed. However, his wife was. Joe had come from the Island of Guam. They settled on Penny Island at the mouth of the Russian River and reared a family. The island supported a garden and a few cows but Joe was principally an inshore ocean fisherman. The congenial Santos was well known and well liked by many people.

It might seem odd that Guerneville families would actually travel to more remote places for a camping vacation, but they did. Jenner was an attractive area, but travel there was most arduous. Parties of teen-age boys and men often traveled by boat. I once made a canoe trip there with Louis Raice. Wagons had to negotiate the steep and somewhat dangerous Monte Rio Grade and Duncans Grade (as we termed the two mountainous impediments from our side). One of my favorite people, Emma "Ma" Dorr, spent the latter half of her life unable to walk because of a spine injury. Her dress caught when the wagon in which she was riding slid off the road at night. She was dragged down a steep embankment.

Joe Santos made irregular trips over the road with a supply of fresh fish wrapped in seaweed. His "fish horn" was a familiar sound as his wagon entered town. Wherever else he tarried, he was certain to stop at the blacksmith shop to exchange happy greetings

---

*Thanks to Dr. Orland Wiseman of Sacramento and Dr. Alfred S. Lewerenz of Hollywood for their separate lengthy replies to my query. This picture and Photo E were copied from deteriorating snapshots in the personal album of Margaret Coon Feliz of Elk.

with Billy Miller. And John Coon was a sort of country squire who could be depended upon for advice or material assistance when needed by people like Joe Santos. At any rate, there the fisherman weighed out and sold his assortment of sea creatures.

And I remember, on just one occasion, a family of Indians, traveling in a light wagon. I am sure they camped overnight in Coon's field, or in the street near the barn. Mostly I remember their loud conversation in a language that somewhat resembled Italian to my ear. I wonder now; was I actually witnessing the very last migration of a Pomo Indian family over the ancient route from the Santa Rosa Valley to the ocean? What a painful and tantalizing thought.

The signs on the front wall of the blacksmith shop generally advertised linaments and ointments to cure all the ills of farm animals. Occasionally there was a notice that some mighty stallion was available for stud service. This was still the age of animal horsepower. But the signs just around the corner on the north side of the smithy were absolutely, incredibly fantastic.

Large circuses, such as Sells Floto, Barnum and Bailey and Ringling Brothers were big yearly attractions in Santa Rosa. And their advance men plastered the rural barns and sheds with beautiful damsels, daringly clad and daringly suspended in the spiderweb of trapeze ropes far above the snarling lions and "taggers" jumping through fiery hoops, and the performing elephants on the ground below. Regrettably, I never had an opportunity to see any of these stupendious spectacles in the flesh; not ever.

Moving to the hardware store one should note the wooden sidewalk so common to most of the town's business area. The low signs there advertise "Mica Axle Grease." The one at Mr. Coon's shoulder recommends "Nason's Pure Liquid Paint." On the telephone pole (and on the Coon palm tree) are signs probably representing political candidates. John ran unsuccessfully for county supervisor against William King of Cazadero. Phil Varner, Mrs. Coon's brother, was a candidate for sheriff.

On display outside the store are a wheelbarrow, manure shovels, horse collars, singletrees, axes and sledge hammers, grindstones and wagonwheel and chicken wire. Inside, to the right, were two rings of buggy whips. Possibly forty whips hung from revolving metal rings near the ceiling. The swinging whips seemed to exude some uncomfortable aura of power and domination that impressed this child.

In these later years he is much more impressed by the memory dating from around age 12 when he could walk into this store with a nickel in hand and ask for five cents worth of gun powder. Mr. Coon would reach down for a black can on the floor under the counter, pour from it a handful of black powder onto the scales and then pour the powder into a small paper bag. Properly wadded into a muzzle loading cannon made of pipe, this explosive could blow an invading enemy fleet right off the face of the river. Guardian angels protected the gunners — most of the time.

I remember Mrs. Robert Garner, who lived across from the smithy, walking her Boston bulldog downtown. And before entering her gate she would say, "Go get your chewing gum." The little dog would dart into the shop, around the legs of stolid draft horses waiting to be shod, pick up an adequate scrap of hoof, and take it home to chew at for maybe an hour.

Garner had come into the community long before my birth to work in woods or sawmill. I knew him as a bartender, generally holding forth at Gori's hotel bar.

That was where most of the local bachelor laboring men roomed and boarded. These were railroad section hands, brush-cutters, and the like. Most, but not all, of these men were "first generation" Italians. By "brush-cutters" we referred to the fellows who gathered and baled branches of redwood and huckleberry and ferns for train shipment to San Francisco florists.

Returning to Bob Garner—his chief claim to local fame unquestionably rested in his interest and success in the game of draw poker. Citizen Garner was also the town constable, a civil position of small honor and considerably less pay. But his official services were seldom needed.

Violence and major crimes were rare in this community. We were, of course, aware of some midnight summer resort rowdyism. And during a couple of summer seasons, the brawling of city toughs at Monte Rio resulted in some equally tough law enforcement measures to stop it. But in our community, during the off-season prior to the First World War, I feel sure I am correct in stating that few household doors were ever locked. The single outside door of the old ranch house in which I was born simply had no locking device until one was installed sometime around 1920, as I remember.

One memorable incident which did bring down upon us a visitation by a very fat deputy sheriff from the county seat was the crazy episode of my peer associate Harry Spencer. Harry dynamited the river. At that time we both must have been about 15 years of age. I watched him from shore as he nonchalantly pushed a blasting cap and about six inches of fuse into half sticks of dynamite. He would light the fuse, push the explosive into a quart fruit jar, tighten the lid, and toss the weighted jar out of his rowboat, all of ten seconds prior to the underwater upheaval.

Game wardens were *persona non grata* in the provincial hinterland of my youth. I knew that it was my tribal duty to forewarn all the clans if I observed one approaching over the near horizon. But dynamiting was frowned upon by the local code. At that particular sporting event, however, I am sure that I tried to persuade Harry that his life, or at least his fingers, were more valuable than the dubious harvest of hardmouth and suckers that were floating belly up around his boat. Oh yes, my adventuresome compatriot eventually paid a substantial fine in court. I have no idea who informed. My own hands were not that clean, so to speak.

Bob Garner was neither a deputy sheriff nor game warden. He represented much of what is right and what is wrong with local community law enforcement ethics and procedures throughout most of the land, and certainly including large cities; there is often a firm and twisted provincialism which ignores the broad statutes of State and Nation.

Bob was a thin, solemn and cadaverous individual who is inseparable in my mind from the legendary gunman of Tombstone, Doc Holliday. I believe that if it had been necessary for Bob to kill a law violator in line of duty he would have done it with as little perturbation as he exhibited whilst drawing to fill a royal flush. Such characters, wherever they enjoyed the respect of the community at large, constituted a vitally important pillar of the frontier community. And Guerneville of that era was essentially a frontier village, although, of course, we were not consciously aware of that.

Beyond the blacksmith shop, to the far right, is the Monticelli villa. I spent many happy hours in the yard there and occasionally in the wine cellar, but never as an imbiber. Mrs. Monticelli would make available slabs of genuine Italian style *pane,* baked in the outdoor "bee hive" oven, but no liquor to minors. They, in company with the other mothers and fathers of my *paesano* companions, called me "Ah-h-Boost," which was their nearest approach to the nickname Buster. One phenomenon that impressed me about this large house was the continuous heavy rumbling from the cellar when wine was fermenting in the great wooden tanks.

I am sure the only lack of courtesy I ever experienced there occurred one day when I walked alone into the yard and deer hound Mindo set his teeth into my lean posterior. I suspect the time was near the opening of deer season, when running hounds are underfed for their own welfare, and they are not to be played with. Thereafter, Mindo and I maintained a cool lack of togetherness.

This malicious, unprovoked assault upon my person, stealthily and from the rear, occurred under the weeping willow tree, a small portion of which may be seen under the hardware store's porch roof. Also here was split and stacked the stovewood which Mr. Monticelli cut and sold as his major business endeavor. The bar and few hotel rooms were rarely, if at all, patronized during the time of my association with son Frank, the youngest child.

It occurs to me that what I refer to as an Italian villa was in itself a phenomenon of the time and place. I give to the Monticelli, Gori and Guidotti domiciles that particular status in our town. A casual observer might have dismissed these large and busy institutions as simply noisy boarding houses with *vino e liquori* as natural accessories. I am more inclined to suspect that they were a sort of cultural stepchild of Medieval Europe, imported with the old country Italians. The need for these hotels seems to have evaporated with the elimination of such heavy labor jobs as had formerly existed in the woods, on railroad maintenance and at the mines.

Beyond the weeping willow tree and backed against the smithy wall was the large, unpainted outside privy. At the end of the yard was the well kept barn with small manure pile adjacent. It should be remembered that the latter by-product was an item of genuine value in a community where back yard (and sometimes front yard) vegetable gardens were common as well as often being objects of prideful exhibit by the householder.

Signor Monticelli, as a youth, had served his mandatory military term in the Italian cavalry. Without doubt this accounted for the sleek and polished appearance of his draft horse and equipment. I had always assumed that similar youthful training in the German army had accounted for the well fed and curried appearance of the matched teams the toil worn and aging Carl Birkhofer used to drive into town every few days from his equally well kept vineyard ranch on the "South Side."

Of course, the livery horses were well fed and attended. I remember especially the dappled mare Stella. She was available for what might now be termed taxi service, with the light rig equipped with red-wheeled, rubber rimmed tires. When Stella trotted out of the wide stable doorway, with Frank Klein or Bill Chambers in firm command of the reins, there was created a picture of flowing perfection which could, I presume, be best compared to a ship under full sail as viewed by a dockside youth of the same era.

Returning to the Monticelli barn and a moment of memorable tragedy there, I remember when the beautiful white mare foundered herself because someone carelessly left a gate open and she had reached a full sack of oats and ate until she died.

I know why a horse turns his rump toward the drifting storm. But I have never learned why he will literally eat himself to death if enough grain food is available. I know why a cow faces the drifting storm. But why, when facing a haystack, will she tear it down and trample and defecate upon it during the process of eating?

Such a question somehow leads one back to the small out-building we hurried past as we left the weeping willow tree. This utilitarian structure looms out of the mist of time as possibly the primary historical milestone separating the departed world of memory from modern rural America. There was no sudden transition from the family two-holer outdoors to a so-called water closet indoors.

Possibly the Monticelli villa, which rose completely anew after the destructive fire of '94, enjoyed a later installation of inside toilet and fixed bath tub. I do not know.

I would guess that about a fourth of the residences in town used outside privies in the year 1910. And so did the school at a much later date. The house I remember as home more than any other, above the church, was constructed 12 or 13 years after the 1894 fire. It was equipped with inside plumbing, including hot water coils in the kitchen wood stove. That decade following 1894 represented a transition period leading out of the long centuries of primitive human waste disposal. And incidentally, households with patent toilets paid 50 cents more than the regular one dollar water bill each month.

During the eleventh or twelfth summer of my life I was employed as general chore boy and baggage smasher at Guernewood Park. I have no recollection of my wage; it was probably about 50 cents a day. One of my prime duties each early morning was the dumping of chloride of lime into the toilet pits throughout the tent camp ground. It is interesting to contemplate whether the strenuous child labor or the community privies would create the greater source of public outrage in our present enlightened age.*

The only other cultural and technological change having a comparative impact during this transition period was the introduction of electric lights in place of candles and kerosene lamps. The gaslit era made a considerable advance beyond candlelight, but it was only in a matter of degree. (The term electric lights

---

It also happened that I was employed in the replacement of the open privies with cesspools and patent toilets. Chris Baagoe and I had a joyous, laborious few weeks on this job. I remember many details of the job, such as nipping wine from the jug that our teamster, Joe Gambetta, thought he had well hidden under some gunny sacks on his wagon. But I cannot place the time. It was in the off-season between 1919 and 1923. The ebullient Baagoe seemed to revel in hard manual labor in spite (or maybe because) of the lack of a lower right arm. Someone later gave Chris an old Model T Ford, but he was refused a driver's license because of his handicap. This was a source of much local amusement because at that time Chris was working for the county as the master manipulator of a manually operated road scraping machine. In fact, idlers used to go out to local jobs to watch him perform.

rather than electric power is favored here because most of the common slave machines of this later day had not yet been invented).

The brief age of illuminating gas never impinged upon Guerneville. Possibly some small and local gas producing equipment was installed, for example at Dan Brian's Nickelodeon. The only incident of this nature that I remember occurred at the Railroad Avenue rear entrance of Dave Hetzel's tobacco store in the brick building. I was probably four or five years old. It was evening and my brother took me there to see the trial run of the new carbide gas production machine.

I don't know when unlimited commercial electric power was available in Guerneville. Probably not earlier than 1915. I believe around 1904 the Guerneville Hotel fired up its own hanging carbon filament globes. The yellow glow had its source in a local dynamo driven by a steam or gasoline engine in some back yard. The result was a small miracle. But this was little more than an indicator of the future importance of electric power.

The Coon home (Photo E) was directly across Fourth Street, north of the Monticelli home. The corner post of the neat fence would indicate Fourth Street extending to the left and west. I suppose the corner would also be the generally accepted end of Cinnabar Avenue and the beginning of the Mines Road going north.

A half-right turn would send one up the hill to the cemetery and about a dozen residences. But it was down-the-hill activity that occasionally took a toll of pickets from the Coon fence. Had there been more motor vehicles than horses the toll of male urchins would unquestionably have exceeded the loss of pickets. One or two boys on a "coaster" could depart the hawk tree, a quarter mile above, and by the time the Catholic Church whizzed by, the Coon fence was looming dead ahead. Consumate skill of the steersman, the Guardian Angel of Small Boys, and a dearth of vehicular traffic all seemed to cooperate in generally delivering the vehicle and its reckless cargo well down Fourth Street toward the Methodist Church.

The Coon home was comfortable, well furnished, and well kept.

For me it reflected both spiritual and physical warmth. In some other residences that I knew the parlor was never a living room. It was utilized to formally entertain very special guests, and most often for the final sad ritual of a family funeral.

Physical warmth was no small matter in this land of frosty mornings and heavy winter rainfall. It was natural that kitchens would become the community living areas at this season. Painful chilblains from cold and wet feet were practically a community wintertime epidemic. Scott's Cod Liver Oil Emulsion helped ward off respiratory ailments, but an application of turpentine could offer only temporary relief to the burning chilblains.

I am not sure if one preventive medicine of my childhood was used to exorcise the Evil Demons of Winter, or if it was blessed by the medical fraternity for some particular purpose. But I do feel that I would be remiss as a chronicler of a bygone era if I did not report upon the asafetida bag I wore around my neck. The dictionary, with scholarly understatement, describes it as "a drug with an offensive odor." I say that them kids which carried the stinking stuff automatically became separated from them what didn't; and that fact probably frustrated the otherwise transfer of a few germs.

Later, during the scourge of the worldwide influenza epidemic of 1918, we again resorted to an odoriferous amulet to preserve us from Unseen Evil. We used a bit of camphor to fumigate our gauze "flu masks". This produced a medicinal smell which bolstered our courage if it did little to discourage the deadly plague.

Our climate was actually delightful both winter and summer if one did not mind a bit of rain and cool humidity. It rarely snowed. In fact, I remember only one occasion when a few inches of snow actually accumulated over the land. This was probably in the winter of 1907-08. I remember it because my father built for me a small sled out of a wooden box. It capsized and I cried because "snow got in my eye." And when I mentioned that to my father along about my twentieth year he was delighted.

"I turned over your sled just so you would remember that day," he said.

The Coon residence was unusual in that it boasted a lawn between fence and house as seen in the picture. Why should a lawn in a front yard be unusual? There was no difficulty in maintaining it. This was a blessed, green land with a great adequacy of sunshine, soil and water. I suspect the lack of domestic lawns could be charged to two general conditions.

This was not an affluent community, even as measured against rural standards throughout California at that time. "Work" meant hard labor, first in the great forest and then on the hillside farms. Garden flowers thrived here with relatively little care. But the very act of maintaining a proper lawn was an indication of urban affluence a little out of harmony with the general draggletailed appearance of this unincorporated village.

Secondly, this was, as stated, a green land which Man had recently violently assaulted. In a very real sense he was still at war with the natural green jungle that would have overwhelmed him if ever he relaxed his labor of chopping, plowing, and stump-pulling.

The Coon porch and yard constituted, therefore, an unusual exhibit of managed verdure. Most unusual were the hanging boxes and pots containing a rare, delicate and beautiful plant, native to a very few damp areas along the North Coast. This was the spidery five-fingered fern.

Behind the house stood the long deserted privy and the barn, and then a garden plot, a small orchard and pasture. During the most severe flood seasons, when the river rose forty feet above normal level, these buildings and the house basement were awash. Some winters were wetter than other wet winters.

The Coon barn deserves particular mention because of its original use. I was told that this structure had housed the shingle and box mill of R. B. Lunsford. Lunsford, the so-called founder and first white settler, owned or had some part in several other mills at various times.

On the Clar Ranch in Mayes Canyon the substantial old barn was likewise said to have been reconstructed upon the foundation of the original sawmill. The logging operation there presumably occurred shortly following the Civil War. A homestead patent to that land was granted in March of 1871 to one Wade H. Sinclair.

Let us return to Cinnabar Avenue of the first years of the Twentieth Century.

There was the day I could have been one of nature's noblemen. The lady was so clearly in distress. I was very young; perpaps less than four. I was stumbling along over the rough board sidewalk near the water trough by the Louvre Saloon. Big brother, maybe 12 years old, was ahead of me. The Ringwalds lived on the southwest corner of Third and Cinnabar. Fred owned the Oak Run Saloon hard by the town end of the river bridge. Mrs. Ringwald's plump Plymouth Rock chickens spent most of the day scratching gravel and horse dung in the street.

The haughty rooster assaulted the defenseless hen practically under my feet. I jabbered a frantic public alarum. But no large persons came to aid me. I am sure the brief memory picture has remained only because I was embarrassed in my confusion. Big brother marched around the corner where the heavy swinging doors of the Louvre banged in and out. And teen-age Ruby Bale giggled as she walked across Cinnabar Avenue.

It was not long after my heroic stance by the water trough that the next episode of Cinnabar Avenue was implanted in my memory bank. It involved my legendary Uncle Frank Clar. This was my first recollection of my father's exciting eldest brother. I saw him only twice thereafter, but his name and local fame were often mentioned by the elders who had known him. The most common reference was to his brilliant mastery of the cornet. And such an accomplishment was no small thing in an isolated village of that era. Uncle Frank had been the town band leader for a time, as had my father.

Frank was a highly intelligent, aggressive business man, generally engaged in lumber or mining ventures. I have been told that his shingle mill, situated about where the last railroad station was later built, was destroyed by fire. It was a rather common occurrence for small mills to catch fire and burn. Just prior to my birth, he and my father operated a shingle mill at Clar's Flat, across the river from Northwood. There stood, and still stands the tallest tree in Sonoma County. I measured it at 339 feet high.

It is difficult to accept all of the tales that I have heard about

Uncle Frank's adventures. For example, he was properly recognized as a great walker. I do believe that he covered on foot a hundred miles of Nevada desert in 23 hours. But my father and others have chuckled over the time Frank is said to have missed the train at Santa Rosa, 22 miles from home. So, quite typically, he began chasing it toward Guerneville. Then the story tellers declare that Frank reached the China House at the east edge of town just as that train was pulling out of town for downriver stations. I wasn't around then. I make no personal deposition. On the other hand, several persons I am inclined to trust told me most positively that Uncle Frank had perfected an electric light prior to Edison's patent.

This driving and somewhat tragic figure apparently found some relaxation in engaging in occasional pranks, such as the little affair which involved me on Cinnabar Avenue. But a much more serious event of that nature had occurred during the first minute of the New Year 1889.

I was a college student when Uncle Frank told me and my brother about the incident. He was laughing all the while he deplored such depraved behaviour upon the part of some person or persons unknown. In fact, one of the town elders told how Uncle Frank had wandered around town on that New Year's Day with a rope and hangman's noose in hand, declaring that he would hang the culprit when he was discovered.

What had happened at the stroke of midnight was a terrific explosion under the old logging locomotive Polly Ann, owned by the Guerne and Murphy Mill. Only the best of good fortune allowed several families nearby to escape injury from flying metal. Several houses were damaged. A relief committee composed solely of George Guerne and Frank Clar provided sufficient funds to repair the damage without any public solicitation.

I must have been an excited little fellow some 18 years after that event when the fabulous Uncle Frank took me down town. There he bought for me a toy walking frog. Strangely, I retain no other memories of that incredible treasure than the short experience on Cinnabar Avenue between the water trough and Count van der Straten's little grocery store.

Uncle Frank had bestowed other treasures upon me. These were about a half dozen large golden oranges. Oranges were a luxury fruit at this time and place. I had probably never held one in my hands before. Now he had taken them out of the paper bag and left the Young Plutocrat struggling to hold all of this impossible armful of Material Wealth. The memory picture is very clear and very brief. There was the laughing man in the middle of the street and the little boy, dropping two oranges in the gravelly dust while trying to pick up one.

When the name Cinnabar Avenue was changed to Armstrong Woods Road the authorities did not seek my advice. Probably I would have suggested such a name as Embarrassment Way.

9

Childhood in a Changing Culture

MUCH of my knowledge of the big world was impressed upon my consciousness by a brother eight years my senior. For example, I am indebted to him for the information that thunder is caused by clouds bumping together. Some meteorological phenomena were revealed to me by my own inherent powers of observation and simplistic deduction. I am sure that I had not reached the age of four when I determined that gusty winds were caused by the tall swaying redwood trees growing on the slope below our home behind the Catholic Church.

Family members used to recall my sitting outside quietly for long periods, obviously meditating upon falling raindrops or falling leaves. From our front porch could be seen the Jones' ranch on the high timbered ridge approximately two miles southwest. On some clear afternoons I would watch the dense ocean fog rolling over that ridge. I could not know that the heavy damp mist, spawned by the cold ocean, had been driven inland straight up the narrow river valley. When it met the sharp turn in the river at Monte Rio the white vapor was pushed up the mountain slope and over the ridge top. But why did the forward face of the great, white, writhing cloud mass then literally disappear into clear blue air? I don't remember having asked any adult why this happened. And I suspect that if I had, the answer would have been of dubious accuracy.

Out of the misty past I present another small story of a kind of cloud. I have rarely told of this incident, and not at all until some thirty years after the event. The reason for my reluctance will be quite obvious.

That incident, and several others, occurred at approximately the same spot. That was a few hundred yards around the hill from where Photo P was taken. Here the south end of Pool Ridge meets the river in the shape of a lightly forested, steep shale rock face. All communication services on the north side of the river between Guerneville and Guernewood Park have to be located upon this sidehill, including railroad, wagon road, power and telephone lines. As a matter of fact, I spent a week or so of very hard and hot labor there working at burying a steel pipe for the water company. I believe that was my "vacation" job for the summer of 1923, after a couple of weeks of working waist deep in water on construction of the local river dam.

The first incident occurred on the railroad trestle along the steep rocky face below the road and above the river. There were three of us boys walking toward town. We were each about twelve years of age and much preoccupied with boy's business on a fine day. Harold Harvey Henry was visiting his relatives, the Cap McPeak family. Twice I warned him that there was danger in walking on the outside trestle stringer. He scoffed at my caution. Then his toe hit a bolt head and he fell headlong. That fall still proceeds through my mind in slow motion. The thud that fractured his skull is no less distinct after so many years. I am sure H. H. H. lived, but I never saw him again after that day when I ran nearly a mile to Doc Schmelz' office.

The next memorable incident to occur at this same place was of little consequence in world history. But it was firmly registered in my mental storehouse. This happened when Jack Hetzel took my BB gun out of my hands and shot the loose gun barrel like an arrow out into the river. He thought that was funny. Of course, he had not expected such a thing to happen. But he had a clothes closet full of toys at home. I did not. So, I suffered a great material loss for a boy living in that cultural environment.*

The third and present subject of interest occurred when I and a couple of companions were standing on the road above the railroad trestle intently watching a silent drama of death across the river. A drowning was not an unknown human tragedy to any of us. We were essentially native creatures of this our beloved green river. In fact, Jack Hetzel's much older brother Carl was a living legend of my youth under just such circumstances. I remember another and much earlier drowning in which Carl was involved. I was a very small boy at the time. Several people were with me in

---

*"And another thing, Jack Hetzel, let's not forget that Sunday morning when we were five years old. I was contemplating the drifting clouds reflected in the mud puddle in front of your house. And you pushed me, face down into the puddle, new sailor suit and all."

deep sand at the edge of the river. I remember the galloping horse pulling the cart down the bank to the beach. The gaunt and sad faced Carl Hetzel stood up in the rolling cart as he began to strip clothes from his lean body. (I am quite sure that he was tubercular). At any rate, no one on the beach spoke, but everyone seemed to point toward the place on the river surface where the unfortunate swimmer was last seen. Carl leaped naked from the cart and dove deep. I cannot report further on this incident. I simply do not remember. But I have paid proper tribute to him who was renowned as the savior of the drowning in a little river town so long ago.

At the time of the principal event of interest Carl Hetzel's body had long since been resting on the hill. I do not remember who were my companions of that day. I am sure we were in the age range of eleven to thirteen years. On the beach across the river the inert body of a young man lay upon the bottom of an overturned boat. Doctor Schmelz walked down the sandy beach to the boat and felt for a pulse beat which obviously was not there. He turned and retraced his steps. The beach was almost deserted and there was silence.

Suddenly an amazing spectacle off to my right attracted my attention. "Look there," I cried to my companions. They declared they did not see anything unusual. I did not try to describe then, or long thereafter, what I had seen.

The day was warm and clear and there was the usual upriver light breeze. What I had seen was a fast-moving, solid, very white, flapping body of something move across the background of vivid green mountainside. It was about the size of a small house. It had no particular shape that I could describe, except that the outside edges seemed more angular than rounded.

A single, isolated and compact wisp of ocean fog could have been there, but only in violation of the natural laws of time, place, and prevailing weather. It could have been a cloud of steam from a railroad engine. But there was no train in the vicinity, and steam would have dissipated in a few seconds on that day. So, it is quite obvious that you should not believe what I say I saw there that brief instant on that tragic summer day after the young swimmer had drowned.

Guernewood Park Entrance, 1912.

The photograph of the rustic entrance of Guernewood Park was made for a commercial postcard in 1912. At that time this campground was probably at the height of its popularity.

Numbered camping sites, rented by the week, were scattered among the young redwoods beyond. A camp unit consisted of a tent on a wooden platform, sheet iron wood stove, burlap stretched around trees for some privacy. Water taps and outdoor toilets were situated throughout the camp area. The dance hall was built over the river bluff above the sandy beach and boat house. Store and boxball "concessions" were near the dancehall. This writer spent the summer of 1912 living at the store concession.
During that vacation season small boys traded crackerjack prize pictures of Coast League baseball players (the major leagues were in a distant world). And they displayed decalcomania transfers of flowers and other things on their skin. Ragtime had just burst upon the fading Victorian world; and this year sunburned swains sang the ditty: "Skinny marink, adink adink, I love you." Practically all well-dressed women had discarded bustles from their wardrobe. William Howard Taft was President of the United States.

Photo J: Miriam District Elementary School.

Photo J presents the school house which must have been regarded with considerable community pride upon its construction early in 1882. The camera is looking southwest. Just when the "little room" (the separate building at left) was constructed and razed I cannot say. I believe both buildings were gone by 1925. This was Miriam District Grammer School. Probably the origin of the name was Old Testament rather than local.

As to the quality of the school house as a teaching facility in my generation, let me quote the expression of an unknown and unexpected visitor one day who sat at a desk at the principal's invitation. In a few moments the visitor arose to leave and muttered, "This building is the damnation of American childhood." Too many elder citizens who had been students here thought differently whenever the subject of a new school was on the election ballot.

In my generation the "big room" (the right or north half of the main building) suffered a crack down the center of the floor. Each half of the floor sloped away from the crack. In winter one husky youth was assigned to feed the cast iron heating stove with chunks of wood to offset the cold ascending from the four feet or more of

119

foundation space. Why the buildings were so raised I do not know. Here the land surface began to slope down to the left to meet the river which was about sixty feet lower; but I doubt if the school yard was ever under flood water.

Black stove pipe was hung across half the ceiling to ascend where smoke can be seen rising at the end of each roof gable. Somehow a cartridge or shotgun cap occasionally found its way into the stove, but not often. This was still the day of severe corporal punishment, and a strap of flexible leather belting hung near the door as a reminder to potential transgressors. My own chief complaint about the structure would be in respect to the miserable reading light afforded by the eight narrow windows for each room. I doubt if electricity was brought into this school even after my departure in 1918.

Before departing from building foundations I must report upon the nether world of the "little room" building. To the left of the lombardy poplar tree (the tree between the buildings was a native pepperwood) was a hole in the bottom siding. During recess, through this hole slid in and out the several regiments of young clod fighters. It is not impossible that the desperate mining for ammunition by the erstwhile holders of the fort eventually did in the old structure by causing the foundation to weaken.

Spinning tops, mumblety-peg with knives, and marble games "for keeps" drifted in and out of season here as they must have elsewhere among school boys across the entire land. At rare intervals we were able to seduce some gullible "city kid" into manning a lonely night outpost with sack and lantern to await the snipe creatures we promised to drive toward him. Sometimes on summer nights we would run through the dark environs of the little village trying to catch a fleet-footed fugitive who was required by the rules of the game to shout "Tally-eye-O" at intervals. Without doubt, this game had its origin in the ancient hare and hounds chase. On the school yard we engaged in our own version of hockey, which we called shinney. The name must have had its origin in the painful fact that the shins of the respective players seemed to register as many blows as the tin can used as a playing puck. Another popular game of similar nature was known as pee-wee. In this case the puck was made of hard wood in the shape of a cigar. It would seem certain that the name originated in the old English word peewit, meaning a cylindrical peg. The game itself seems to have disappeared.

Two other popular school games were called Red Line and Black Man for no particular reason. The games had something to do with trying to run over a line scraped in the dirt across the school yard. Very possibly these games originated far back in history, as did the more gentle ring- around-the-rosy ritual played by the girls over on the other side of the building. "High-O-the Cherry-O, the farmer chose a wife."

We played baseball, too. In fact, this field saw several inter-small-town contests. Our dire poverty in baseball equipment led directly to an interesting joint effort which could not have been duplicated in many schools. Behind, and to the right of the camera, near the boys' privy, was a noble redwood stump. It must have been ten feet in diameter, six feet high, and very solid.

We kids clambered up the spring-board notches left there by the choppers, maybe forty years earlier. Those of us who held the summit were Kings of the Mountain.

This stump constituted a decided handicap for any baseball center fielder. So we considered its removal by boy power. Principal David Lockton was enthusiastic and he negotiated with the board of trustees for us to deliver and pile stove wood chunks in the school woodshed. I have forgot the sum of money involved, but it was at the going rate for fuel wood. Nor do I remember where we borrowed double-bit axes, sledges and wedges, crow bar and cross-cut saw.

The boys involved were between the ages of eleven and fourteen. Probably all of us were responsible for such chores at home as splitting stove wood. A few of the hillside farm lads looked upon school time as vacation from work. We knew how to use the tools, and equally important, we knew how to avoid injury. The project was a success. We ended with a level field, a new catcher's mit, a bat and several "dollar and a quarters", which meant, of course, professional quality baseballs.

The steps and entrance hall in the center of the big building was duplicated on the girl's side. Hall doors led off to the middle and

121

big rooms. In my time, four grades sat together in each room. The "little room" was not in use for lack of students. I believe total enrollment was about 65. In the entry hall was a large zinc trough served by a cold water faucet and one tin drinking cup. On the wall was hung a roller towel for all comers. I remember Mr. Lockton standing before the 4th to 8th graders one morning with a very dirty roller towel in hand. "And here it is now only 9:30 in the morning," he said.

School was very serious business. I ranked high in scholarship and avoided the leather strap. But I never enjoyed school at any level at any time. It must have been a miserable experience for some very slow learners who were presumed to be simply indolent. Staying after school an hour was common punishment. I endured that for a month for simply refusing to appear for a special singing excursion. The experience was probably beneficial; ever since it has caused me to have some sympathy for rebels.

One kid who licked the system very briefly was Francis Howe. The Howe brothers, with Alfonse Gonfiotti used to walk nearly three miles from across and down the river at Clar's Flat. Francis used to tend his trap line en route. One morning he was careless with a captured skunk. Francis came out of it with a beautiful skunk pelt and a pungent, nauseating aroma that surrounded him like an invisable deadly cloud. He was firmly instructed to spend that day outside the school at a respectful distance from all humanity.

Of the little room I have only one outstanding memory. The time was very surely the early afternoon of Friday, December 17 1909. I was not yet a student. Older brother had received permission to take me to a special Christmas party. I remember the excitement at being allowed to sit with a much older girl (who was actually decidedly homely). There was a douglasfir Christmas Tree (which would have been known only as pine in that community). It was decorated with fluffs of cotton, strings of pop corn and a few trinkets, with numerous small colored candles burning.

I don't remember much of the party. Without doubt, this was the first such affair I had ever witnessed. But I do vividly remember Santa Claus coming in with his bag of toys. He was padded and dressed in the best tradition. Unfortunately, his clothes were trimmed with white fluff cotton. I remember his stooping over near the tree to retrieve a toy. A blue flame streaked away from a candle over the body of Santa Claus.

I was pretty much caught up in the near panic after that and don't remember what happened. I heard that the Pool boys, Buzz, Jake and Bullfrog went out the window nearest the poplar tree. Santa Claus was a cigar maker named Dunn who worked for Dave Hetzel. Principal W. P. Frost tried to beat out the flames after pushing Santa into an anteroom. Both men suffered painful burns.

Photo Ja: School children Memorial Day parade about 1912.

Photographs Ja and Jb could well have been taken on the same day. They record the typical small town recognition of Memorial Day in the early Twentieth Century. All of the deceased, and especially the soldier dead were remembered this day.

As I recollect these exercises I am inclined to wonder if present day America is not in effect more embarrassed by its dead than indifferent. A show of patriotism has, of course, become a very different matter. I make this statement as historical fact and without editorial comment. Yet, I cannot leave that statement without reference to the flagpole in the picture. (Incidentally, the gentleman in the derby hat is not known to me).

At one time the halyard, that is, the flag rope, became fouled at the top of the pole. After retired Navy officer, Lee R. Boland, who lived at Guernewood Heights, asked why no flag was flying he promptly agreed to unfoul the line. Boland was deaf and going blind because of an explosion aboard ship years earlier. His personal heroism had saved several lives then.

We boys watched and admired his ascent up the pole by the use of short ropes around his body and the flag pole. He unfouled the line and pulley and descended in the same nimble manner. Principal David Lockton (who can be recognized by his bald head at the far left of Photo Jb) said to Boland, "No amount of money could have hired me to do that job."

"Nor me." said the patriot. "I did it for my country."

It is obvious that the unknown photographer gathered the girls for Photo Ja. My sister Imelda and Margaret Coon are seen immediately behind parade leaders Jack Hetzel and the tall Gilbert Trosper. Jack was my age, and he would naturally assume some leading role in these affairs. I suspect that the bunch of flags in his hand were to be placed on the graves of military veterans when we arrived at the cemetery.

It would seem that the smaller girls would not be expected to walk the mile, mostly uphill, to the cemetery. On the contrary, my sister remembers that her chief concern during the rest at the last sharp turn in the road (between Peterson's vineyard and Billie Oberfell's apple orchard) was the red dust gathered on her white shoes.

The young man in the picture center background was "Milkie" Maloof. His parents operated an ice cream store on Railroad Avenue. They were Turkish immigrants. Above him were branches of the eucalyptus trees that lined the entire school lot on the Main Street side. In the center background is the Ben Peugh residence at the corner of Church and Main. To the right across the street was Noel Tunstall's undertaking parlor.

Our generation was still living under the shadow of the great Civil War that had occurred forty and more years earlier. Perhaps this was more the fact in small towns than in the cities. Many of our morning songs in school were such lugubrious selections as "Glory Hallelujah" and "Tenting Tonight on the Old Camp Ground, Waiting for the War to Cease." Such doleful hymns plus my highly sensitive and shy nature must have developed the dislike for group singing that has never left me. Yet, there I was, back to the camera, in Photo Jb, with the tip of the flag directly behind my shoulder.

Sergeant David Hetzel, of New York's 74th Infantry Regiment, quite naturally always seemed to me to be a very old man. He was short, bow-legged, white haired with a wispy white goatee. He always wore a black campaign hat and a small lapel button which probably indicated his membership in the Grand Army of the Republic. Although Dave had immigrated from Germany in his youth, he spoke English with a definite accent. He was congenial, witty, and I dare say, stubborn when necessary. I faintly remember his tobacco plantation under the bridge (before Smith built the Theatorium) and his drying yard at the Hetzel home on the northeast corner of Fourth and Mill streets.

Of my numerous memory pictures of Mr. Hetzel, the most pleasant relates to his gift to me of the three Melachrino Cigarette cardboard gentlemen. These smiling dandies wore white tuxedos with top hats and canes. The cut-out, stand up advertisements were about a foot high. This precious gift of utterly insignificant intrinsic value was made one evening when I went to the shop on Main Street with my father to buy a tin-foiled package of Dixie Queen pipe tobacco.

Several days before each Memorial Day Old Dave would come to the school to give us a very loose drill preparatory to our marching to the cemetery. "Left Wheel, right wheel, in column of twos." Sometimes he would relate incidents of wartime, such as his place in an honor guard for President Lincoln.

Photo Jb: At the cemetery on Memorial Day about 1912.
The author is third from right, the flag tip at his shoulder.

At the cemetery, in Photo Jb, the weather was obviously warm and bright. The small boys give the appearance from the rear of wishing they were elsewhere and out of their "best" clothes. Several are in bibbed overalls. Mrs. Esterling, a sister of Antionette Cobb, is in the center, bonneted and leading us in doleful song. We no doubt had already heard some wordy speeches about Appomattox Court House. The year must have been 1911 or 1912.

On the day, a half-dozen years later, when Sailor Jack Coon was carried up the hill behind a pair of matched blacks carrying jet black plumes on their collars, we, the community, were present and closer to our military dead. And we felt then that we were sure of the cause of their going.

Photo K: The railroad depot prior to 1935.

Photo K shows the second and last railroad depot and freight shed which was occupied in 1912. This was between Mill Street and Church. The hand pulled truck at right was rolled next to the baggage car to transfer outgoing and incoming baggage and mail. There was an inside waiting room as well as outside benches. The busy Mr. Martin was the first station master of my recollection. His family were our near neighbors on the hill.

Near the women in the picture is the ticket office. This protruded so that visibility up and down the track was afforded the station official. Off the picture to the left was the semaphore signal mast. I don't remember about freight trains, but regular passenger trains gave the usual two long, two short whistle blasts at the edge of town. The station master dropped the signal arm, saying: "Come in and tarry awhile." And the engineer would toot-toot "Thank-you." It all seemed quite unnecessary. But then, commuting high school kids were nuisance enough without being allowed to change operating rules.

Throughout the summer days this place was a beehive of activity. Before automobiles had become common, in the 1920's, there were often extra trains called special sections. They flew

127

green flags at either side of the headlight to indicate their special status.

All day, and all night too, I suppose, the telegraph instrument in the office clickety-clacked. No one seemed to pay any attention until the local call clicks alerted the otherwise indifferent station attendant. For years this was the commercial telegraph message center for this village and other towns served by railroads. Every few months the station master would remove old blue acid from the several square glass battery jars and clean and replenish them. His electric power supply was entirely that local.

Across the track, left of the picture was Blake's Ice Cream Parlor, under the trees of Westover's planted forest. Later Blake's moved north to where Fourth Street crossed Fife Creek, and angled across from Guidotti's Garibaldi Hotel.

Both the social and business activity around a small town railroad depot have been mentioned. Another cultural aspect of the railroad should be noted. Without radio, television or easy mobility over the poor roads, the railroad was an obvious communication channel with the outside world. For many of the young men of such communities, whether or not they recognized the fact, to become an engine wiper and eventually an engineer, or a brakeman and eventually a passenger conductor was a way out of town and into the big outside world.

Photos M and L move progressively east up Railroad Avenue from the railroad station. The three pictures are practically continuous. These are train-time crowds of "summer people." The soldier in uniform, walking the rail sets the date at approximately 1919 or earlier.

The Laws family operated the Ice Cream Parlor and Box Ball Bowling Alley. The sign for the alley is behind a cork elm tree. This same tree is seen in Photo L to the left of the post office. That was the structure which was nearly a victim of the 1919 fire.

Box ball was a popular commercial pastime of the era. "Pins" were hinged, and those scored by hits were reset by the pull of a lever. The game has apparently disappeared in favor of the current popular free pin bowling sport. Incidentally, at the time of the picture there was a modern bowling alley across the street at the

Photo M: Laws' Ice Cream store and boxball alley at Railroad and Church Street, about 1918.

Photo L: The post office about 1918.

former Maloof (later Laws) establishment. (Around 1930 the Grove Dance Hall was constructed there). Also, more directly across the street in the 1917 era stood Saule Gori's saloon and hotel and the adjoining Italian bocci ball court. The general renovation of Railroad Avenue after the 1919 fire greatly altered the old town in this area. The neat and modern Bank of Sonoma County was constructed in 1922 at the corner of Church Street on the former site of the ice cream parlor.

Community groups of mankind the world over and throughout all time have changed in the spirit and behavior of their daily lives; sometimes very slowly, and sometimes rapidly. That very small portion of earth surface that came to be called Guerneville has noted several distinct cultural eras.

There were the long centuries when the land was lightly touched by the aboriginal Indians. The theoretical control by Russians, Spaniards and Mexicans, prior to the timber harvesters, passed around the wilderness, causing hardly a ripple upon the lower Russian River waters. Then there was the brief period of the timber harvesters.

With the elimination of the high timber, the great hope of America of that day became evident. Strong men struggled to create family subsistence farms upon the naked land. The soil and the climate responded well, but not to equal the rich abundance of the hot, flat, well-watered agricultural valleys of Interior California.

Contemporaneously with the creation of the vineyards, and prune and apple and hop ranches, there was initiated the strange idea of urging city dwellers to come and recreate along the river and under the second-growth redwoods. A half century earlier in national history such a venture would not have been conceivable. The predominantly rural population did not "take vacations" as a matter of privilege. In the case of the lower Russian River country, easy railroad accessibility from San Francisco was a major factor in the success of the recreation economy.

The availability of commercial electric power caused an abrupt step, almost a lunge forward away from the old culture. Yet, I strongly believe that the family acquisition of automobiles created the greatest modification of the life this writer observed about him in his childhood and youth.

Public use and demand caused the construction of new roads and the paving of old routes. I happened to have been standing at the south end of Guerneville bridge on May 7, 1927, and saw the first load of cement dumped on the first paving project of Pocket Canyon Road. No longer would the plodding two horse teams haul river gravel to spread over this roadway every few years in the age old ritual of country road maintenance.

Eventually, the town streets were covered with black top. No longer could small barefoot boys squish the fine street dust, flavored with powdered horse dung, up through their bare toes in summer time. No longer could they taunt Ed Smith by running behind his daily water wagon tours, challenging him to catch them in the fountain spray that gushed from the rear as he played his foot pedal controls from the driver's seat.

The increasing movement of commodities and "summer people" to and from the river resort area by truck and auto caused other changes. It eventually caused the railroad to cease operation. In the heyday of the train transportation, the vacationers could not move about so easily. Boarding resorts such as Murphy's, Neeley's and Bert Guerne's Southside Farm were very popular. There were many others operated on a smaller scale. Eventually they closed. The age of the summer cottage and the motel had matured. People purchased their own household supplies in town, and the camp ground deliveries ceased to operate.

The town, the people, and the core culture of my youth have departed. Such was inevitable in the relentless flow of Time. The forested hills remain. The ever-living residual redwoods push themselves upward once again into the blue sky. The gentle summer river flows seaward between the folded hills. Through it all this, my homeland, has existed as a most favored bit of our Mother Earth.

Looking north from Neeley Hill in 1958. Two photos meet along the ridge of Lone Mountain in middle distance. At far left, Pool Ridge slopes down to a barn on the Big Bottom where Livreau sawmill stood a century ago. At upper left corner of cleared flat is the mouth of Forgotten Valley. Hidden over the hill lies Armstrong Grove. Skyline summit above is "The Gillum". In 1883 David F. Gilliam homesteaded there in the East Austin Creek drainage. Pat Devine homestead (Luttrell Ranch) and site of Summit School are on this left center skyline. At extreme right is Mt. Jackson fire lookout. Lower, at bottom of cleared firebreak is the cemetery. At lower right corner the river beach is visible. Congregational Church steeple (center of right photo) marks Old Main St. near Church. In mid-distance a few redwoods still show the effect of the 1923 fire by their narrow crowns.

Photo Ne: Taken by the author in 1958 from near Laws' house. The familiar school belfry is no longer there, and the town is compacted.

ACKNOWLEDGEMENT

The Foreword tells the intent of this writing. Yet the most important guiding precept can be found there only in inference. That was my determination to write about subjects of my own choice, and in the manner that pleased me. This was a labor of love in which I was dominated by the feeling that I myself was to be the primary audience. Obviously, old photographs furnish a flexible structural core for the writing. The whole thing actually started as a descriptive caption for a picture of the 1919 fire rubble. But descriptions of old pictures, laced with sometimes irrelevant reminiscenses of the author, constitute a fine recipe for literary chaos. I did, however, try to maintain some chronological order to the general flow of events.

For the pre-American period I borrowed from a talk I delivered at the Guerneville Chamber of Commerce dinner meeting in the too late evening of January 30, 1970, and which was subsequently printed in the Santa Rosa *Press Democrat.* Also, I borrowed some ideas and words I had written about the early movies for the 1970 winter issue of *Sonoma County Historical Journal.*

In this labor, my sister and brothers were interested and very helpful. The intensive editing of the manuscript by my wife Evelyn and Esther Gall resulted in the general improvement of the entire writing. And as the text indicates, this story benefited much from the notes, old photos and conversations with the late Julia Guerne. We talked several times at her Santa Rosa home in 1958. She was 88 years of age then, and confined to a wheelchair. But her personality was still as peppery as it had been so long ago when she was my boss during the Guernewood Park employment.

"Home folks" whom I called upon were always anxious to peer into the misty past and find answers to sometimes vague questions. I wish to thank Jim Neeley, Lincoln Stewart, Lenabelle Miller, Frances Perdue, Jack Hetzel and Maud and Harold Laws. Annie Laughlin King, who probably shares my earliest dim memory of the Maypole dance so long ago, and her husband Tom were good enough to read the entire manuscript to assure that dreams and half forgotten gossip did not enter the story as historical fact. Margaret Coon Feliz made valuable comments regarding the draft of the chapter titled Cinnabar Avenue. Mrs. Ann Sullivan, a busy Sacramento librarian, was kind enough to read the manuscript at my behest, for the purpose of viewing it as a reader with no acquaintance with the events or the people.

Some of the photographs not credited must have been the work of Newton Lark or Johnny Parkins. Originals of those noted in the caption by a (JPD) are fortunately deposited in Healdsburg City Archives. They were the work of professional photographer Joseph P. Downing. I am very grateful to city official Edwin Langhart for their use.

County Recorder Herb Snyder and his staff at Santa Rosa contributed valuable assistance during my research there. The State Library at Sacramento offered, as usual, a great treasure house of records and documents.

From the beginning I was encouraged and helped by my friend and advisor, professional printer Ralph Ahlgren. For typing, paper shuffling and devoted interest in this very personal publication I thank friends Dorthy McGill and Raymond Tatian.

This book was set in 12 point Aldine Roman type and printed at Cal Central Press in Sacramento.

CRC.
Sacramento
June 1973